Contents

Introduction

Acknowledgements

Every effort has been made to contact the holders of copyright material, but if any here have been inadvertently overlooked the publishers will be pleased to make the necessary arrangements at the first opportunity.

How to Use the Materials

Icon Explanations

Test Your Understanding – following key points and definitions are exercises which give the opportunity to assess the understanding of these core areas. Within the work book the answers to these sections are left blank, explanations to the questions can be found within the online version which can be hidden or shown on screen to enable repetition of activities.

Illustration – to help develop an understanding of topics and the test your understanding exercises the illustrative examples can be used.

Quality and accuracy are of the utmost importance to us so if you spot an error in any of our products, please send an email to mykaplanreporting@kaplan.com with full details.

Our Quality Co-ordinator will work with our technical team to verify the error and take action to ensure it is corrected in future editions.

Exam Introduction

To complete the CIMA qualification and be able to use the designatory letters of ACMA and CGMA, candidates for this prestigious award need to achieve three things:

- attain the entry requirements for the professional level qualification
- study for and complete the relevant professional level assessments and examinations
- complete three years of relevant practical experience

This text concentrates on the second of these requirements, and in particular to study for and complete the Operational level case study exam.

Overview of exam

The integrated case study exam will be available four times a year. The purpose of this exam is to consolidate learning at each level by reflecting real-life work situations. The exam is human marked.

This approach allows a wide range of knowledge and skills to be tested including research and analysis, presentation of information and communication skills whilst still ensuring competence in key skills.

CIMA believe that this new format will provide the commitment to delivering the competencies which employers desire thereby improving 'employability'.

For example, the Operational level case study exam will be set within a simulated business context, placing the candidate in the job role matched to the competency level. In the case of the Operational level, the job role is that of a finance officer (usually a management accountant) with responsibility for some of the consequences of implementing strategy. The focus will be on the short-term.

Typical aspects of such a role could include the following:

- An understanding of costs and cost accounting, in order to start preparing budgets, and to advise about short-term changes in products, volume and prices.

- Putting budgets together for the business also requires an understanding how the business is structured, and will require communicating aspects of the budget to non-finance staff; both in the preparation and the delivery.

- Preparation of financial reports to show how the business is performing. This will require knowledge of the regulatory environment, financial reporting, and business taxation.

- Analysing and advising on working capital, cash and short-term finance.

The exam is intended to replicate "a day in the life" of a finance professional operating at the operational level and provide a simulated environment for candidates to demonstrate the required level of proficiency in each of the competency areas. Consequently, the exam will be set and marked according to the competency weightings at the level.

The integrated case study exam is 3 hours in duration and is made up of a series of timed tests or tasks. This makes the case study exam different from most exams you will have sat to date – once you have submitted a particular task (or the time limit is reached, whichever is sooner) you will be moved on and will not be able to return to that task. This should reduce the problem of not completing the paper but does mean you will need to be very disciplined when attempting each task.

Candidates will be provided with access to pre-seen information approximately seven weeks before the real exam.

Assessment aims and strategy

The integrated Case Study examinations combine the knowledge and learning from across the three pillars of the syllabus set in a simulated business context relating to one or more fictional business organisations which are in turn based on a real business or industry.

The integrated case study is three hours long. The case study will include both pre-seen and un-seen material, the latter being made available during the examination. They will incorporate short written answers, emails, letters and any form of appropriate communication required within the tasks set.

The focus is on application, analysis and evaluation which are levels 3, 4 and 5 of the CIMA hierarchy of verbs (see below).

Simulated business issues in the integrated case studies provide candidates with the opportunity to demonstrate their familiarity with the context and interrelationships of the level's technical content. This reflects the cross functional abilities required in the workplace. Skills will include research, analysis, presentation of both financial and non-financial information and communication skills.

Feedback will be provided to candidates with their results. Exam sittings for the case studies will occur every three months. Candidates must have completed or be exempt from the three objective tests at a particular level before attempting the relevant integrated case study.

Learning outcomes

Each syllabus topic from the objective test subjects contains one or more lead learning outcomes, related component learning outcomes and indicative syllabus content. This provides a guide for the likely content of the case study exam.

Each lead learning outcome:

- defines the skill or ability that a well-prepared candidate should be able to exhibit in an examination

- is examinable and demonstrates the approach likely to be taken in examination questions

The lead learning outcomes are part of a hierarchy of learning objectives. The verbs used at the beginning of each learning outcome relate to a specific learning objective as illustrated in the detail below. You will not necessarily see these verbs reflected in the case study requirements but they indicate the depth of knowledge required for particular topics. Requirements in the case study may be presented as requests for reports, presentations, etc, as well as simple tasks. The case study exam will focus on Levels 3, 4 and 5.

Level 1

Learning objective – Knowledge (What you are expected to know)

- List – Make a list of
- State – Express, fully or clearly, the details/facts of
- Define – Give the exact meaning of

Level 2

Learning objective – Comprehension (What you are expected to understand)

- Describe – Communicate the key features of
- Distinguish – Highlight the differences between
- Explain – Make clear or intelligible/State the meaning or purpose of
- Identify – Recognise, establish or select after consideration
- Illustrate – Use an example to describe or explain something

Level 3

Learning objective – Application (How you are expected to apply your knowledge)

- Apply – Put to practical use
- Calculate – Ascertain or reckon mathematically
- Demonstrate – Prove with certainty or exhibit by practical means
- Prepare – Make or get ready for use
- Reconcile – Make or prove consistent/compatible
- Solve – Find an answer to
- Tabulate – Arrange in a table

Level 4

Learning objective – Analysis (How you are expected to analyse the detail of what you have learned)

- Analyse – Examine in detail the structure of
- Categorise – Place into a defined class or division
- Compare and contrast – Show the similarities and/or differences between
- Construct – Build up or compile
- Discuss – Examine in detail by argument
- Interpret – Translate into intelligible or familiar terms
- Prioritise – Place in order of priority or sequence for action
- Produce – Create or bring into existence

Level 5

Learning objective – Evaluation (How you are expected to use your learning to evaluate, make decisions or recommendations)

- Advise – Counsel, inform or notify
- Evaluate – Appraise or assess the value of
- Recommend – Propose a course of action

How to use the material

These Official CIMA learning materials brought to you by CIMA and Kaplan Publishing have been carefully designed to make your learning experience as easy as possible and give you the best chances of success in your Integrated Case Study Examinations.

This Study Text has been designed with the needs of home study and distance learning candidates in mind. However, the Study Text is also ideal for fully taught courses.

The aim of this textbook is to walk you through the stages to prepare for, and to answer, the requirements of the Case Study Examination.

Practical hints and realistic tips are given throughout the book making it easy for you to apply what you've learned in this text to your actual Case Study Exam.

Where sample solutions are provided, they must be viewed as just one interpretation of the case. One key aspect, which you must appreciate early in your studies, is that there is no single 'correct' solution.

Your own answer might reach different conclusions, and give greater emphasis to some issues and less emphasis to others, but score equally as well if it demonstrates the required skills.

If you work conscientiously through the official CIMA Study Text according to the guidelines above, as well as analysing the pre-seen information in full, you will be giving yourself an excellent chance of success in your examination. Good luck with your studies!

Planning

To begin with, formal planning is essential to get the best return from the time you spend studying. Estimate how much time in total you are going to need for each subject you are studying for the Case Study Examination. You may find it helpful to read "Pass First Time!" second edition by David R. Harris ISBN 978-1-85617-798-6.

This book will provide you with proven study techniques. Chapter by chapter it covers the building blocks of successful learning and examination techniques and shows you how to earn all the marks you deserve, and explains how to avoid the most common pitfalls.

With your study material before you, decide which chapters you are going to study in each week, which weeks you will devote to practising past exams, and which weeks you will spend becoming familiar with your case study pre-seen material.

Prepare a written schedule summarising the above and stick to it! Students are advised to refer to articles published regularly in CIMA's magazine (Financial Management), the student e-newsletter (Velocity) and on the CIMA website, to ensure they are up to date with relevant issues and topics.

Tips for effective studying

(1) Aim to find a quiet and undisturbed location for your study, and plan as far as possible to use the same period of time each day. Getting into a routine helps to avoid wasting time. Make sure that you have all the materials you need before you begin so as to minimise interruptions.

(2) Store all your materials in one place, so that you do not waste time searching for items around your accommodation. If you have to pack everything away after each study period, keep them in a box, or even a suitcase, which will not be disturbed until the next time.

(3) Limit distractions. To make the most effective use of your study periods you should be able to apply total concentration, so turn off all entertainment equipment, set your phones to message mode, and put up your 'do not disturb' sign.

(4) Your timetable will tell you which area to study. However, before diving in and becoming engrossed in the finer points, make sure you have an overall picture of all the areas that need to be covered by the end of that session. After an hour, allow yourself a short break and move away from your Study Text. With experience, you will learn to assess the pace you need to work at.

(5) Work carefully through each chapter, making notes as you go. When you have covered a suitable amount of material, vary the pattern by attempting a practice exercise. When you have finished your attempt, make notes of any mistakes you made, or any areas that you failed to cover or covered more briefly.

(6) Make notes as you study, and discover the techniques that work best for you. Your notes may be in the form of lists, bullet points, diagrams, summaries, 'mind maps', or the written word, but remember that you will need to refer back to them at a later date, so they must be intelligible. If you are on a taught course, make sure you highlight any issues you would like to follow up with your lecturer.

(7) Organise your notes. Make sure that all your notes, calculations etc can be effectively filed and easily retrieved later.

(8) Attempt practice exercises and write out full answers. Reviewing these and reflecting on suggested solutions is a crucial part of your studies.

Relevant practical experience

In order to become a Chartered Global Management Accountant (ACMA, CGMA), you need a minimum of three years' verified relevant work-based practical experience.

Read the 'Applying for Membership' brochure for full details of the practical experience requirements (PER). At the time of print CIMA were in the process of updating these requirements for 2015.

Information concerning formulae and tables will be provided via the CIMA website, www.cimaglobal.com, and your EN-gage login.

Introduction to case study exams

Chapter learning objectives

- To gain an overview of the case study exam, its purpose, structure, marking and process involved.

1 Why a Case Study Examination?

The Case Study Examination is an attempt to simulate workplace problem solving, and allows examiners to move one step closer to the assessment of competence than is possible with objective test questions. It is a test of your professional competence.

CIMA wishes to assess:

- your possession of skills such as research, synthesis, analysis and evaluation, in addition to

- your technical knowledge, and

- your skill in presenting and communicating information to users.

Since the examination tests a range of different skills, preparing for this examination needs to be different from studying for a 'traditional' examination. The purpose of this text is to suggest how you might prepare for the examination by developing and practising your skills.

2 Your role

Each case study exam will be set within a simulated business context, placing the candidate in the job role matched to the competency level.

In the case of the operational level the job role is a finance officer, typically a management accountant, reporting to first line managers and/or peers within the organisation.

The competency level is described as "entry-level", requiring the candidate to demonstrate the ability to analyse and advise on various aspects and consequences of the implementation of strategy.

3 CIMA's Competency Framework

CIMA has developed a competency framework which explains the skills which a finance professional needs to possess in order to drive their organisation forward. This framework highlights the importance of not just accounting techniques but also wider business management skills. It also emphasises the need for complete integration of these many and varied skills. It is no longer sufficient for a finance professional to only display relevant technical ability.

The technical competencies are still important but in addition the accountant must have a good understanding of the organisation, it's environment and other relevant commercial knowledge. It is also important to possess the relevant people and leadership skills to ensure that technical and business knowledge is applied appropriately and effectively throughout the organisation.

The four generic competencies can be summarised as:

(1) Technical skills ('Do accounting and finance work')

(2) Business skills ('In the context of the business')

(3) People skills ('to influence people')

(4) Leadership skills ('and lead within the organisation')

CIMA recognise that the relevance of each of these competence areas will depend on the level a professional has progressed to within the organisation.

So for an entry level role (broadly equivalent to operational level), the technical skills will form a large part of the role and only a small amount of leadership skill will be expected. This is reflected in the syllabus weightings.

As you progress from operational to management level it is anticipated that your role is more in line with a manager and therefore you will be expected to display a greater understanding of the business context and have developed more people and leadership skills. At the strategic level the weightings for each of the four areas of competency are equal, reflecting the fact that as a senior manager you need to balance a broad range of skills.

Whilst the objective tests will examine your knowledge and ability to apply the underlying technical, business, people and leadership skills, the case study exam aims to test your ability to demonstrate and integrate these skills as a rounded finance professional.

4 How the Case Study Examination works

The Case Study Examination is a computer-based examination of three hours.

Candidates cannot take the examination until they have successfully completed all the Objective Test Examinations for the relevant level. The exam comprises a series of requirements, which aim to integrate and apply the technical knowledge tested in the Objective Test Examinations.

(a) Triggers – information and updates regarding situations in which the company finds itself

(b) Tasks – work you will need to carry out based on the trigger

The exam is based on:

- pre-seen material issued in advance of the exam day, supplemented by

- additional, previously unseen material given to you in the exam room.

5 The pre-seen

CIMA releases the pre-seen material approximately seven weeks before the examination. This is posted on the student area of the CIMA website (www.cimaglobal.com) and it is your responsibility to download it and to print off a copy.

The pre-seen material is an introductory scenario to set the scene for the case study, together with accounting and financial information. Much of the financial information will probably be in the form of appendices to the main text, but the main text of the pre-seen might include some figures too.

The pre-seen material is an extended scenario consisting of approximately 6 exhibits giving information about a business organisation. You will be taking on the role of a management accountant who works for the organisation, and your responses to the tasks will usually be addressed to your superior.

The pre-seen information for the pilot exam (which concerns MW – a manufacturer of animal feed) comprises:

- Exhibit 1 – Overview
  - General Background
  - Sales and customer history
  - Purchases and supplier information
  - Accounting and costing systems used by MW
  - Current market conditions and new Research and Development facility
  - MW results and position
  - MW's employees
- Exhibit 2 – an article on MW's animal feed
- Exhibit 3 – standard cost cards
- Exhibit 4 – a newspaper article concerning MW
- Exhibit 5 – a set of financial statements
- Exhibit 6 – a report from an industry body

As you can see there is information relevant to all three operational level technical subjects.

The purpose of giving you access to this information in advance of the exam is to enable you to prepare notes, analyse and become very familiar with the organisation(s) and industry described. Remember, you have the role of a management accountant within this organisation and so you should use the pre-seen material to get a similar background knowledge as would be expected from someone in this situation.

Suggested approach to analysing the pre-seen information

(1) **Detailed exhibit by exhibit analysis**

As you review each exhibit ask yourself questions about what each piece of information means and what the implications of it might be for the organisation. Try to consider why the examiner might have provided this information.

(2) Technical analysis

Now it's time to apply many of the techniques you studied for the Objective Test Examinations to help you understand the organisation and the industry in which it operates in more depth. Some suggestions of what you could perform:

- Ratio analysis of financial statements and financial plans.
- Business strategy analysis, including generation of strategic options.
- Management accounting analysis, including costing, pricing and performance measurement.

(3) Researching the industry involved

At the operational level included within the pre-seen material there will be industry data and information, which could be presented in a variety of ways. This data and information should be reviewed alongside the information about the company.

Whilst industry data will be provided, you might find it helpful to undertake your own research into the industry to provide background and depth to your understanding.

(4) Ethical analysis

An analysis of the ethical issues facing the organisation now and a consideration of those which could arise in the unseen material.

(5) Overall position analysis

Once you have completed all of the above, you should be able to stand back and see the bigger picture of the organisation within the case material. You should complete a position audit, including a SWOT analysis so you have a clear understanding of where the organisation is and where it might want to go.

(6) Identification of key issues

Using your SWOT analysis, you should now be able to identify a short list of key issues facing the organisation. An appreciation of these will assist you when understanding the issues introduced in the unseen material in the exam.

6 The unseen

In the examination you will be provided with:

- an on-screen version of the pre-seen material
- additional unseen material, which contains both triggers (new information) and tasks (what you need to do)
- an on-screen calculator
- space to complete your answers

The unseen material will be a continuation of the pre-seen and will usually bring the scenario up to date. In many cases there is a 'twist' in the unseen i.e. a development that students might not have anticipated from the pre-seen. The unseen may focus on a number of issues that appeared in the pre-seen or it may just focus on one or two; either way it will provide the basis for the content of your answers.

A common mistake made by weaker students is that they place too much emphasis on their analysis of the pre-seen material and do not develop the information in the unseen material adequately. The key points to be referred to in your answer should be driven by the new information in the unseen material.

7 Triggers

Each section in the unseen material will begin with a **trigger**.

This will be information provided as an introduction to the work that you are required to complete.

The information may be in the form of a briefing by your superior, a newspaper article, some financial information or extracts from internal reports. You will be expected to integrate this new information with the analysis you have performed on the pre-seen material to produce a coherent and well informed response.

Here is an example of a trigger from the pilot exam:

Example trigger from pilot exam

Four weeks later, after your annual leave, you return to work to find the following email from Mr Harris:

From: Mark Harris, mh@mw.co.uk
Sent: 27th July 2015
Subject: Factory

Welcome back from your annual leave – just thought I'd update you on what's going on.

To put you in the picture I completed on the purchase of the factory last week and we are now in a position to fit out the space ready to commence production. As you already know the factory itself cost £1,500,000 which has been paid for out the finance raised from a new bank loan. On top of that we have so far paid £700,000 for plant and equipment and £150,000 for professional fees out of our available cash. The rest of the plant and equipment (approximately £800,000) will need to be paid for. We are a profitable business and we should have enough cash to cover this, even if it means using our £250,000 overdraft facility temporarily.

The production manager expects that we will start production on 1 October and that we will make our first sales to the national animal feed distributer in the middle of October on 60 day credit terms. We currently have 30 day credit terms with our suppliers.

Mark Harris
Director
MW
E: mh@mw.co.uk
T: 0151 266 3114

As a result of the email that you received on 27 July 2015, Mr Harris asked you to prepare a cash flow forecast for the next five months. You ascertain that on 1 August 2015, the balance in the bank was £400,000. You completed the cash forecast on 3 August 2015 and sent it to Mr Harris.

Your forecast can be accessed using the reference materials button above.

8 Tasks

Within each section of the examination, there will be a task or tasks that you will be asked to perform, usually by your superior. These tasks will require different types of response, although usually reports and emails.

There is a time limit attached to each task. Once you have submitted a task (or the time limit is reached, whichever is sooner) you will not be able to return to that task. This should reduce the problem of not completing the paper but does mean you will need to be very disciplined when attempting each task. Time management is discussed in further detail in Chapter Eight.

The pilot exam comprises the following requirements:

- A report covering how an activity based costing system (ABC) differs from a traditional absorption costing system; the advantages and disadvantages to the business of using ABC; the implication of using ABC on costing information; and the likely difficulties the firm might encounter switching to ABC (P1).

- An email covering the effectiveness of online recruitment and alternative methods (E1) and advice on how a new property asset will affect the financial statements and it's effect on the profit of the firm in the future (F1).

- An email covering the benefits of setting more formal budgets and the different approaches to budget setting that might be appropriate for the firm. As part of this you were required to explain the types of individual budget that might be appropriate, giving examples of the information required to create them (P1).

- An email discussing the implications of a cash flow forecast (F1) and advice concerning B2B marketing and the use of key account managers (E1).

Here is an example of a task from the pilot exam (note this task follows on from the trigger shown on the previous page):

Example task from pilot exam

Upon receipt of the cash flow forecast Mr Harris becomes concerned and sends you the following email to which you need to respond:

From: Mark Harris, mh@mw.co.uk
Sent: 4th August 2015, 11:26 a.m.
Subject: Cash flow forecast and marketing

Thank you for the cash flow forecast that you sent through to me. I am a little alarmed and perplexed though that the forecast seems to show that we will breach our overdraft facility limit. Firstly, why is the position so bad? Secondly is there anything that we can do to improve the cash position so that the overdraft limit isn't breached?

On a related matter, given this cash position, the effective marketing of our products is becoming a major consideration, in that we need to ensure that the new factory is utilised to near it's full capacity. In order to effectively market our products I've heard from a friend that we need to engage in business to business marketing, and perhaps employ a key account manager although I'm not clear how this differs from any other type of marketing. Please can you advise how this might help the business?

Thank you

Mark Harris
Director
MW
E: mh@mw.co.uk
T: 0151 266 3114

9 Marking of the Case Study Examinations

9.1 Competencies

The Case Study Exams will be marked against the competencies summarised in section 2 of this chapter.

For the operational level the weightings applied to these competencies are shown in the following diagram:

OPERATIONAL LEVEL

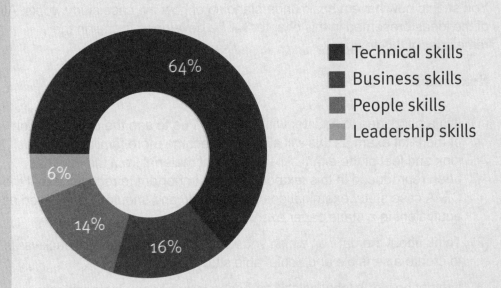

- ■ Technical skills
- ■ Business skills
- ■ People skills
- ■ Leadership skills

As you can see there is significantly more focus on technical and business skills and less emphasis on developing your people and leadership skills. This reflects the syllabus content for the exams within the Operational level.

The following two chapters will explain further how these competencies relate to each syllabus. You can also see in Chapter 11 how the competencies are applied in the marking of the pilot paper.

9.2 What you need to do to pass overall

There are **two** criterion that must be met to pass overall.

(1) Students must score over 60% overall.

   The overall mark is a "scaled" score based on the maximum marks available.

(2) Students must score at least 33% of the marks available for each competency.

At operational level, the leadership and integration marks do not count towards this criterion but that still leaves the additional requirement of having to get at least 33% of the marks for technical, business and people skills.

However, it is important to note that CIMA have advised students to focus on answering the requirements set rather than worrying about picking up marks for each competency. Marking guides are designed so that, if you answer the requirements set, then you will achieve the level of individual competency marks needed.

10 Summary

You should now have a basic understanding of how the case study works. All of the ideas presented in this chapter will be developed further in the remainder of this textbook.

Next steps:

(1) It is a good idea to register with Pearson Vue to see the online version of the Pilot exam as this will allow you become more familiar with the look and feel of the exam. All the relevant material from the Pilot has been reproduced in this textbook but it is important to recognise that the CIMA case study examinations are dynamic and shouldn't be viewed as equivalent to a static paper exam.

(2) Think about the date on which you will sit the exam and work backwards to create a sensible and achievable study timetable.

(3) It might be worth locating and gathering together any materials you already have from the supporting technical subjects (E1, P1 and F1). We will show you in later chapters how you may need to use these materials.

Understanding competencies

Chapter learning objectives

- To understand how the learning outcomes from individual papers can be interpreted in terms of the competencies required for the case study exam.

1 Relevance of the Operational level syllabus

Let us start by revisiting the key learning outcomes covered in the three individual Operational level papers and consider how the learning outcomes could be relevant within a case study scenario.

E1 – Organisational management

Syllabus area A: INTRODUCTION TO ORGANISATIONS (25%)

Chapters of the CIMA text	You must be able to....	Additional information
1 – The different purposes of organisations	• Discuss the different ownership and motives of organisations • Discuss mission and vision • Discuss how an organisation creates value for its stakeholders	Possible area for case study may be appraising the achievement or appropriateness of an organisation's mission
2 – Organisational structure	• Explain Mintzberg's organisational configuration • Explain the different types of organisational structure and structural dimensions • Explain different organisational forms and functional boundaries, such as offshoring and outsourcing	Possible areas for case study may be the recommendation and justification of an appropriate structure or an evaluation of an offshoring or outsourcing decision

| 3 – Governance, regulation, ethics and CSR | • Discuss the purpose and principles of good corporate governance

• Discuss the creation of an ethical organisation and the principles of corporate social responsibility

• Discuss the impact of regulation on the firm

• Discuss the development of business-government relations | Prime areas for case study could be advice on how to deal with an ethical situation where maybe you are being asked to go against some of the principles, explaining what threats you face and the necessary action you should take to deal with the issue

In addition, may ask for an evaluation of a socially responsible approach |

Syllabus area B: MANAGING THE FINANCE FUNCTION (15%)

Chapters of the CIMA text	You must be able to....	Additional information
4 – The purpose of the finance function	• Analyse the components of the finance function • Explain the activities fundamental to the role of the finance function • Discuss the potential for conflict within the role of the finance function	Prime areas for case study could be advice on how to structure the finance function or on the different activities carried out by the finance function
5 – The contemporary transformation of the finance function	• Explain the key changes in the finance function and the reasons for these changes • Discuss some of the key changes such as offshoring, outsourcing and BPR in more detail	Prime areas for case study could be an evaluation of the use of offshoring or outsourcing for the finance function and recommendation of suitable alternatives such as internal outsourcing or near-shoring

Syllabus area C: MANAGING TECHNOLOGY AND INFORMATION (15%)

Chapters of the CIMA text	You must be able to….	Additional information
6 – The purpose and management of the technology and information function	• Evaluate a new IS • Discuss systems development with a particular focus on testing, changeover and maintenance • Discuss the change management issues associated with IS implementation • Discuss privacy and security and ethical issues • Discuss IT enabled transformation such as homeworking, virtual organisations and teams	Possible area for case study may be advising on the management of the change management process (for example, using Kotter, Schlesinger and Sache) or the evaluation of the use of homeworking or virtual companies/teams
7 – Emerging IS trends and their role in supporting organisational strategy and operations	• Discuss e-business • Discuss knowledge management systems and customer relationship management systems • Discuss trends such as wireless technology, cloud computing, social media and Big Data	Possible area for case study may be advising on the benefits and uses of Big Data (this could also be tested in the context of the marketing section of the syllabus)

Syllabus area D: OPERATIONS MANAGEMENT (15%)

Chapters of the CIMA text	You must be able to....	Additional information
8 – The purpose of the operations function	• Discuss the use of Porter's value chain • Discuss the different sourcing strategies available • Distinguish purchasing from supply with a link to Reck and Long's strategic positioning tool and Cousins' strategic supply wheel • Discuss process design and improvement techniques • Discuss sustainability and CSR in operations	Prime areas for case study could be an evaluation of the strategic significance of the operations function or a discussion of relevant sustainability and/or CSR issues associated with an operations function
9 – Tools and techniques of operations management	• Discuss techniques for managing operational capacity, forecasting demand and managing inventory • Explain the types of process technology • Discuss layout and flow • Explain work study • Discuss the importance of quality and the techniques of quality management • Discuss lean management • Explain the importance of reverse logistics	Prime areas for case study would be recommendations of methods for improving operations management. These may range from the implementation of new process technology, to the implementation of a quality approach

Syllabus area E: MARKETING (15%)

Chapters of the CIMA text	You must be able to....	Additional information
10 – Introduction to marketing	• Define the marketing orientation and the alternatives to it • Understand the marketing environment, e.g. using PESTEL • Discuss consumer behaviour, including the decision making process, theories, factors affecting buying decisions and types of buyer behaviour	Possible area for case study may be a discussion of current approach to selling products and the recommendation of a marketing approach
11 – The market planning process and the marketing mix	• Describe the market planning process • Discuss segmentation, targeting and positioning • Explain what is meant by the marketing mix and explain each element separately and in detail • Discuss the importance of branding • Discuss the use of Big Data in marketing	Prime case study question will focus on one or more of the 4P's or may examine branding
12 – Further aspects of marketing	• Describe the differences between B2B and B2C marketing • Explain internal marketing • Discuss marketing sustainability, ethics and social marketing • Discuss marketing in a not-for-profit context	Prime case study question will focus on the differences between B2B and B2C marketing or the ethical/CSR issues associated with marketing

Syllabus area F: MANAGING HUMAN RESOURCES (15%)

Chapters of the CIMA text	You must be able to....	Additional information
13 – An introduction to human resource management	• Define HRM and discuss the HR planning process • Discuss recruitment, selection or induction	Prime areas for case study could be distinguishing between a soft and hard approach to HRM, an evaluation of the different selection methods or a discussion of the purpose and contents of an induction programme
14 – Appraisal, training and development, motivation and retention	• Explain the steps in, types of and barriers to appraisal • Distinguish learning training and development with a focus on Kolb, Honey and Mumford and Kirkpatrick • Discuss the types of and aims of a reward package • Describe the importance of workforce flexibility • Discuss knowledge workers, employee involvement and psychological contracts	Possible case questions may focus on appraisal barriers and solutions or an evaluation of the different reward systems
15 – Employment practices, HR roles and ethics	• Explain the issues associated with fair and legal employment • Discuss the role of the line managers and HR professionals • Discuss ethics and HR	Possible case questions may focus on redundancy or dismissal issues or how to deal with ethical dilemmas at work

P1 – Management Accounting

Syllabus area A: COST ACCOUNTING SYSTEMS (30%)

Chapters of the CIMA text	You must be able to....	Additional information
1 – Traditional costing	• Discuss the advantages and disadvantages of marginal and absorption costing • Apply marginal and absorption costing in respect of profit reporting and inventory valuation, including the reconciliation of budget and actual profit • Explain the issues that arise in pricing decisions and the conflict between 'marginal cost' principles and the need for full recovery of all costs incurred	• Examining marginal or absorption cost cards and explaining how each could be used to determine a selling price for a product • Explain the impact of each system on profits and inventory values
2 – Activity based costing	• Compare and contrast activity based costing with traditional marginal and absorption costing methods • Explain the reasons for the development and need for ABC	• Explain the benefits that ABC might bring when compared to traditional costing methods • Explain the impact that a change to ABC might bring to a business

3 – Other costing techniques	• Explain how product selling price might be impact by the method used to apportion joint costs • Explain throughput accounting • Categorise different types of environmental costs	• Highlight potential environmental costs that may be impacted by new process or strategy • Explain the concept of throughput and its usefulness for decision making
4 – The modern manufacturing environment and the importance of quality	• Explain why quality is becoming more important to industries • Explain TQM and JIT, their pre-requisites and their advantages and disadvantages • Categorise quality costs	• Discuss how standard cost cards, reported profits, financial statements etc. might be impacted by a switch to TQM and/or JIT • Consider whether TQM or JIT would be suitable to the organisation under consideration
8 – Variance analysis: calculations	• Illustrate how budgeted and actual profit or contribution is reconciled	• Calculations are unlikely to feature in the case study. However, you could be given a reconciliation and asked to comment – see below

9 – Variance analysis: discussion elements	• Link variances to their causes • Explain the limitations of variances in modern production environments • Explain how variances can be applied to service industries	• Review an operating statement and comment on the performance of operational managers • Use a variance report to highlight operational issues for an organisation • Suggest variances that could be used in a service industry • Explain how variances might change under different costing systems (e.g. marginal, absorption or activity based costing)
10 – Variance analysis: advanced variances	• Explain the meaning of mix, quantity and planning variances • Discuss the limitations of the methods used	• Review an operating statement and comment on the performance of operational managers • Use a variance report to highlight operational issues for an organisation • Suggest variances that could be used in a service industry • Explain which variances might change in the presence of revisions to the original plan • Explain the meaning of and rationale behind mix/yield and operational/ planning variances

Syllabus area B: BUDGETING (25%)

Chapters of the CIMA text	You must be able to....	Additional information
11 – The budgeting framework	• Explain the purposes of budgeting • Interpret budgets • Discuss the advantages and disadvantages of rolling budgets • Discuss the advantages and disadvantages of incremental budgeting • Discuss the advantages and disadvantages of zero based budgeting • Discuss the advantages and disadvantages of activity based budgeting	• Evaluate the suitability of a specified budgeting approach • Discuss the impact of changing to a different budgeting system • Criticise an existing budgeting system • Highlight problems evidenced in budgets (e.g. from a cash budget) • Discuss the impact of a change in a budget variable
12 – Budgetary control	• Explain the difference between feedback and feedforward control • Discuss the advantages and disadvantages of budgetary participation	• Highlight problems which have arisen due to budgetary participation • Recommend a level of budgetary participation
13 – Forecasting techniques	• Discuss the advantages and disadvantages of linear regression • Discuss the advantages and disadvantages of time series analysis	• Determine whether or not a method is appropriate given past patterns in data and expected changes in the organisational environment

Syllabus area C: SHORT TERM DECISION MAKING (30%)

Chapters of the CIMA text	You must be able to....	Additional information
5 – Break-even analysis	• Calculate the break-even point in single and multi-product situations • Calculate the margin of safety • Understand the assumptions in the technique • Interpret cost-volume-profit diagrams	• Provided with a diagram, explain critical points such as the break-even point or margin of safety • Consider other factors to consider when launching a new product • Consider the achievability of a margin of safety
6 – Relevant costs and decision making	• Explain which costs should be considered for different types of decisions	• Make decisions based on provided cost data • Consider other factors to consider when making decisions
7 – Linear programming	• Explain the difference between slack and surplus • Explain the meaning of a shadow price • Discuss the limitations of the linear programming technique	• Interpret linear programming constraints • Interpret a linear programming solution • Make suggestions based on a linear programming solution

Syllabus area D: DEALING WITH RISK AND UNCERTAINTY (15%)

Chapters of the CIMA text	You must be able to....	Additional information
14 – The treatment of uncertainty and risk in decision making	• Explain how different attitudes to risk lead to different types of decisions • Discuss the limitations of expected value techniques • Explain the difference between perfect and imperfect information	• Make decisions based on different risk attitudes • Comment on the usefulness of the technique used to make a decision

F1 – Financial Accounting

Syllabus area A: REGULATORY ENVIRONMENT FOR FINANCIAL REPORTING AND CORPORATE GOVERNANCE (10%)

Chapters of the CIMA text	You must be able to....	Additional information
6 – The regulatory environment	• Identify the need for regulation • Identify the key duties of the international bodies	• Possible area for case study advising on the different ways a country can implement an accounting regime, i.e. adopt IFRS or use a local system
7 – The conceptual framework	• Explain the key principles of The Conceptual Framework for Financial Reporting issued by the IASB	• Possible area for case study advising on the principles of the Conceptual Framework in relation to a specific accounting transaction

8 – External audit	• Identify the objective of external audit • Identify the different types of audit report • Explain the duties and rights of auditors • Explain the benefits of an audit	• Possible area for case study advising on an appropriate audit report with reasons or advising why an external audit would be beneficial to an entity
9 – Ethics	• Identify the Code of Ethics principles and threats • Explain how to deal with an ethical dilemma	• Prime areas for case study could be advice on how to deal with an ethical situation where maybe you are being asked to go against some of the principles, explaining what threats you face and the necessary action you should take to deal with the issue
10 – Corporate governance	• Identify the need for CG • Explain the methods of CG	• Possible area for case study advising on the methods of CG you could adopt and the advantages or disadvantages of each

Syllabus area B: FINANCIAL ACCOUNTING AND REPORTING (45%)

Chapters of the CIMA text	You must be able to....	Additional information
2 – Accounting for investments in subsidiaries and associates	• Define the rules of control, significant influence • Identify the difference between a subsidiary and an associate with appropriate treatment • Understand general terminology for group purposes	• Prime areas for case study could be advice on how to deal with an investment in the consolidated financial statements, i.e. should it be an associate or subsidiary, why should it be treated this way and how do we account for it
3 to 5 – The consolidated statement of financial position, the consolidated statement of profit or loss and associates	• Prepare consolidated financial statements for a parent, subsidiary and an associate • Deal with inter-company trading, inter-company balances, unrealised profit • Deal with the valuation of NCI using the proportion of net assets method or fair value and the impact this has on impairment	• Prime areas for case study could be advice on how to deal with adjustments in the consolidated financial statements, i.e. how should they be accounted for, where would they be adjusted for, what would they have an impact upon
11 and 12 – Introduction to single entity accounts and statement of cash flows	• Prepare the financial statements for a single entity	• Possible area for case study interpreting a statement of cash flow and explain the importance of it

13 – Non-current assets	• To identify capital and revenue expenditure and appropriate treatment • To account for the purchase, disposal, depreciation, impairment and revaluation of an asset • Prepare the non-current asset note • Understand the rules of IAS 16, 23, 36, 38	• Possible area for case study advising how to treat an item and explaining why, i.e. capitalise with reasons or expense with reasons, revalue or impair with reasons – applying the rules of the appropriate accounting standard
14 – Non-current assets held for sale and discontinued operations	• Identify and value an asset held for sale • Identify a discontinued operation • Understand the rules of IFRS 5	• Possible area for case study advising how to treat a discontinued operation or asset held for sale
15 – Government grants and investment properties	• Identify the difference between a capital and revenue grant • Account for all types of government grants • Account for investment properties using the cost or fair value method • Understand the rules of IAS 20 and 40	• Possible area for case study advising how to treat a capital or revenue grant for the first time or as a repayment • May also be asked to discuss accounting issues surrounding investment properties
16 – Misc standards	• Understand the rules of IAS 2, 8, 10, 34 and IFRS 8	• Possible area for case study advising how to treat an item in the accounts, i.e. is it an error, estimate or change in policy as per IAS 8? What is a reportable segment in a scenario?

17 – Accounting for tax	• Understand the rules of IAS 16 • Account for current tax and under and over-provisions	• Possibly mix this topic with syllabus area D asking how to account for a tax charge for the year
18 – Foreign currency	• Understand the rules of IAS 20 • Understand the rules for initial recording of a transaction, year end adjustments and payment • Identify the difference between a monetary and non-monetary item	• Possible area for case study advising how to treat an item in the accounts, i.e. to identify if it needs adjustments depending on whether it is monetary or non-monetary
19 – Employee benefits	• Understand the rules of IAS 19 • Identify the difference between a defined benefit and defined contribution scheme with accounting entries	• Possible area for case study advising how to treat an item in the accounts, i.e. is the scheme defined benefit or contribution?

Syllabus area C: MANAGEMENT OF WORKING CAPITAL, CASH AND SOURCES OF FINANCE (20%)

Chapters of the CIMA text	You must be able to….	Additional information
20 – Short-term finance and investments	• Identify the different types of finance and investments and the advantages or disadvantages of using them	• Possible area for case study advising the sources available and the advantages or disadvantages of using them, maybe evaluating different options

21 – Working capital management	• Identify the objectives of WC • WC policies • The WC cycle • WC days calculations	• Possible area for case study advising the different approaches to WC such as the aggressive model, advising on how to reduce the cycle and impact this will have on the business, explanations of the changes in WC days and what they mean
22 – WC receivables and payables	• Collecting debts – methods and aged receivable analysis • Factoring and invoice discounting • Offering/taking discounts	• Possible area for case study advising the advantages or disadvantages of various methods, explaining different methods an entity could use
23 – WC inventory	• Inventory levels and implications – advantages and disadvantages • EOQ calculations	• Possible area for case study advising the inventory level of an entity and implication of high or low levels
24 – WC cash	• Cash budget calculations • Cash models	• Possible area for case study interpretation of a budget, advising on improvements

Syllabus area D: FUNDAMENTALS OF BUSINESS TAXATION (25%)

Chapters of the CIMA text	You must be able to....	Additional information
1 – Fundamentals of business tax	• Define the general terminology of taxation • Define the difference between different types of direct and indirect taxes • Calculate direct taxes for trading profits and capital items • Understand the methods of loss relief for trading and capital items • Understand the general administration process of taxation including the powers of tax authorities, sources of rules, evasion and avoidance • Understand the concept of residency, general types of foreign tax and the methods of gaining double taxation relief	• Prime areas for case study could be advice on how to deal with an item for tax purposes, e.g. explaining how loss relief could be applied, the residency rules

2 Introduction to case study competencies

Seeing all the learning outcomes set out like this can be intimidating, especially if you feel overwhelmed and not sure how to pull everything together into a structured approach. To help get a sense of perspective it is vital that you bear in mind the following:

• You will not be asked to perform detailed calculations within the case study exam as these will be tested rigorously in the OTQ exams. However, you might need to undertake simple calculations to support your discussions.

- While all syllabus areas can, and will, be examined in multiple scenarios, many tasks will focus on the "core" areas from P1, E1 and F1. So for example, within P1 this would mean budgeting, costing, variances and short term decision making.

- Finally, for the case study exam, the individual paper learning outcomes are augmented/supplemented by four generic competencies to aid focus.

As we explained in Chapter 1, at this level you will be tested on those competencies expected of a finance officer, such as a management accountant.

The weightings for the generic competencies at operational level are:

- Technical skills – 64%

- Business skills – 16%

- People skills – 14%

- Leadership skills – 6%

OPERATIONAL LEVEL

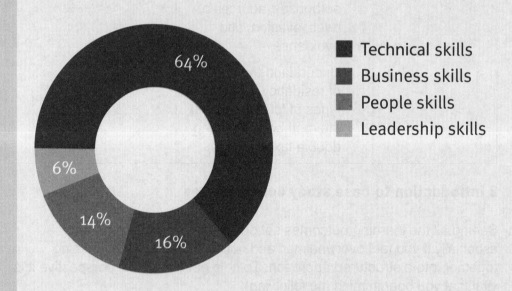

So you will be expected to show core technical skills such as advising on various possible courses of action (after relevant analysis) from your P1 paper ('doing accounting and finance work') whilst taking into account the wider business context such as your understanding of the marketing environment from E1 ('in the context of the business'). You may then need to make decisions and communicate them using techniques learnt in P1 and E1 ('to influence people') and potentially advise on managing the resulting change process using skills learnt in E1 ('whilst leading within the organisation').

Note: at the operational level 'influencing people' is really limited to the practical aspects of influencing, such as effective marketing, the ability to effectively change systems and so on. The psychological aspects of 'change' and 'influence' are dealt with in E2.

You should aim to be comfortable with the whole syllabus for all three subjects and should be ready to attempt the whole paper as there is a limit to the extent to which strength in one topic can compensate for weakness in another.

Let's examine each generic competency in more detail before thinking about integrating these skills. Remember a competency focuses on what you can DO rather than what you KNOW and so you need to think about this in terms of ability rather than simply knowledge.

3 The case study competencies in more detail

The generic competencies and individual paper learning outcomes can be correlated as follows:

CIMA COMPETENCY FRAMEWORK

Competencies	Syllabus area		
Technical skills	E1	P1	F1
Financial accounting and reporting			F1
Cost accounting and management		P1	
Planning and control		P1	
Management reporting and analysis		P1	
Corporate finance and treasury management			
Risk management and internal control		P1	
Taxation		P1	F1
Accounting information systems	E1	P1	F1
Business skills			
Strategy			
Market environment	E1		
Process management	E1		
Business relations	E1		
Project management			
Regulatory environment			F1
Macro-economic anlaysis			
People skills			
Influence			
Negotiation			
Decision making		P1	
Communication	E1		
Collaboration and partnering	E1		
Leadership skills			
Team building			
Coaching and mentoring			
Driving performance			
Motivating and inspiring			
Change management			

Underpinned by ethics, integrity and professionalism

This can be discussed in further detail as follows:

3.1 Technical skills

At the operational level these skills will be drawn predominantly from subjects P1 and F1, with P1 being the main driving paper for this level.

Here is a sample of some of the competencies which you may be expected to demonstrate (note: this list should not be taken as exhaustive but is here to give you more of an idea how the case study works):

- I can evaluate and recommend different costing systems (P1)

Illustration 1

Scenario/Trigger

F Company is a family run business specialising in the manufacture and sale of bridesmaid dresses. It has recently extended its product range to include dresses for six form student proms, accessories, hair dressing services, tanning and nail bars. The accountant is struggling to price products as F does not currently use a full absorption system for costing items.

Task

Discuss the arguments for and against implementing a full absorption costing system.

Suggested approach

- Make a note of all of the possible advantages and disadvantages of absorption costing verses marginal costing

- Decide which are these arguments are particularly relevant for F.

- Consider the practicalities – what types of fixed costs might be faced by the company, the different possible methods for absorbing them and how this could work for F – for example, a rate per hour approach may be appropriate for hand made items but not for bought in accessories.

- Check whether the requirement extends to making recommendations – if so, then you could also consider alternatives such as ABC.

- I can evaluate and recommend different budgeting systems (P1).

Illustration 2

Scenario/Trigger

B Company is a rapidly-expanding consultancy service. unfortunately the rapid growth has resulted in various problems, ranging from consultants being double-booked, to massive overspends on work for certain clients and unexplainable losses on others. B currently uses an incremental top down system of budgeting.

Task

Evaluate the budgeting system at B and make recommendations for improvement.

Suggested approach

- Make a note of all of the possible advantages and disadvantages of incremental v ZBB and top down v bottom up approaches.

- You could also note down the main objectives of budgeting – control, authorisation, communication, etc.

- Decide which are these issues are particularly relevant for B – for example, there is clearly a lack of control over spending – can you identify why this has happened?

- Decide which aspects of a typical budgeting system need improving – allocation of responsibility, target setting, participation, etc.

- Make a clear recommendation – for example, to appoint budget holders for different parts of the business.

- Note: try to think beyond just the P1 aspects here – relevant E1 issues could include the possible need for a change in organisational structure (say to divisional) or the need for a new MIS to facilitate the new budgeting system.

- I can interpret a variance analysis statement and make recommendations to improve performance (P1)

Illustration 3

Scenario/Trigger

For many years V Company has operated a number of care homes for the elderly. To facilitate growth it has recently opened a hotel that is open to the general public. At the management meeting at the end of the first quarter the team was presented with a variance analysis report that showed a large number of adverse variances. The Operations Director has warned staff that if this continues then most of the team will fail to be awarded bonuses.

Task

Some of the team feel the current system is unfair and you have been asked to evaluate the performance management system at V and make recommendations for improvement.

Suggested approach

- Use your P1 knowledge to get an overview of the current system by looking at key elements of the process – how standards were set, how responsibility was allocated, what targets were set, whether the budget was flexed appropriately before calculating variances and so on. For example, if standards have been set based on experiences with care homes, then they might not transfer easily to a hotel.

- For each variance – particularly adverse ones – try to identify cause and effect from the information given. In particular see how responsibility can be allocated or whether or not variances were due to factors out of managers' control. For example, if guest numbers were much higher than forecast, then there may have been a need for overtime payments to cleaners to ensure quality. The cleaning manager should not therefore be penalised for a cost overspend.

- Make clear recommendations – for example, that the first quarter will be a settling in period so a less aggressive tone should be taken by the Director.

- I can explain decisions based on pay-off tables and apply the different criteria of expected values, maximax. maximin and minimax regret (P1).

- I can explain a break-even chart and concepts such as contribution, break-even point and safety margin (P1).

- I can interpret a key factor analysis calculation and advise on a production plan given constraints (P1).

Illustration 4

Scenario/Trigger

R Company runs a number of large retail outlets on an out-of-town retail parks around the country. During the next two months the one particular shop will be having refurbishment work done that will halve the available floor space. Rather than simply reducing the volume of all products in inventory, a colleague has suggested using key factor analysis to rank products according to the contribution they generate per square metre of shelf space used.

Task

Advise the store manager on the usefulness of key factor analysis in this case and discuss other relevant factors to be considered.

Suggested approach

- Make a note of as many limitations or assumptions of key factor analysis as you can from your P1 knowledge.

- Make a note of other factors that affect sales demand and product decisions, say from your knowledge of E1 marketing.

- Look for clues in the pre-seen and unseen to help apply and assess the different arguments. It is often easiest to identify reasons why a suggestion might fail – for example, whether certain products are typically bought together so one cannot be ranked before the other, whether some products may be considered to be loss leaders so would rank poorly but are vital to other sales, etc.

- Try to step back from the technical content and use common sense to see if there are any other practical issues that can be brought into the discussion – for example, if orders have already been placed in advance with suppliers, then revising the sales mix may be problematic.

- I can advise on different methods of analysing and managing operations (E1)

- I can advise on different methods of improving quality within operations (E1)

Illustration 5

Scenario/Trigger

F company manufactures cuckoo clocks. It has recently lost market share due to both pricing and quality issues so is considering modernizing some of its operations and introducing quality practices. The Operations Director recently came back from a conference where quality costs and six sigma were mentioned but not explained.

Task

Explain what are meant by 'quality costs' and 'six sigma', what is involved in implementing six sigma and the likely benefits and problems that may result for F.

Suggested approach

- Make a note of the different costs of quality – prevention, appraisal, internal failure, external failure

- Give examples of each in the context of F

- Make a note of all of the pros and cons of six sigma

- Decide which are particularly relevant for F looking in detail at its circumstances.

- I can assess a firm's working capital position and make recommendations for improvement (F1)
- I can recommend techniques to manage a cash surplus or a deficit (F1)

Illustration 6

Scenario/Trigger

X company has produced a cash flow forecast that indicates a deficit in 6 month's time that will last for a further 3 months. Debt factoring has been suggested as a potential solution.

Task

Evaluate the use of debt factoring and make recommendations.

Suggested approach

- Make a note of as many advantages and disadvantages of debt factoring as you can.

- Look for clues in the pre seen and unseen to help apply and assess the different arguments – for example, the minimum time period that a factoring arrangement could be set up for, the likely cost, the effectiveness of the company's credit control function, etc.

- Consider alternatives and evaluate their suitability – e.g. would invoice discounting be better as a short term solution?

- I can understand and interpret consolidated financial statements (F1)
- I can explain and apply relevant international accounting standards (F1)

Illustration 7

Scenario/Trigger

G company is considering building a new factory to facilitate growth and is considering whether or not to apply for a local government grant to help finance the expansion. The project manager is unsure as to the impact of the grant on the financial statements.

Task

Discuss the impact this grant is likely to have on the financial statements of G.

Suggested approach

- Decide what type of grant is involved i.e. revenue or capital.
- Recap the treatment of grants according to IAS 20.
- Consider impact on Statement of Financial Position and Statement of Profit or Loss.

3.2 Business skills

At the operational level the skills within this generic competency fall mainly within the E1 syllabus with some also coming from F1 and P1.

Here is a sample of the competencies which you may be expected to demonstrate:

- I can discuss the most appropriate techniques for managing organisational relationships (E1)

- I can analyse the structure of an organisation and make recommendations (E1)

Illustration 8

Scenario/Trigger

F company has traditionally made and sold just one product line in its home country. The Directors have decided to expand the range of products sold and look to grow through sales into foreign markets and have now tasked business unit heads with identifying critical areas where F may need to change for the plan to be implemented successfully. F currently has a functional structure.

Task

Evaluate the current organsational structure of F and make recommendations.

Suggested approach

- Note down the different structural options available – functional, divisional and matrix – and their relative advantages and disadvantages.

- Consider the specific circumstances of F to see which of the advantages and disadvantages of functional structures are currently being experienced and which new structure would fit best – for example, it might be easier to ring fence investment in new products if a divisional structure is implemented.

- Make clear, justified recommendations.

- I can coach and mentor staff (E1)

- I can participate in driving organisational performance (E1)

- I can motivate and inspire staff (E1)

Illustration 9

Scenario/Trigger

X company is about to embark on a comprehensive programme of upgrades to its information systems that will have particular relevance to the finance department.

Task

Draft an email explaining these changes to the department.

Suggested approach

- Think about how these changes will affect the department – what will their main concerns be?

- What will the benefits be to the department?

- Address the above two points in your email using a positive tone.

- I can discuss how a costing or budgeting method may be suitable for a particular company (P1)

- I can discuss whether decision-making techniques, such as thoughput, may be beneficial in a particular situation (P1).

- I can identify other factors that may be relevant to a decision, given the wider context of the organisation (P1)

- I can discuss the impact of the regulatory environment of an entity (F1)

3.3 People skills

At the operational level the skills within this generic competency fall mainly within the E1 syllabus with a small amount also coming from P1 (decision making).

Here is a sample of the competencies which you may be expected to demonstrate:

- I can discuss the concepts involved with managing people

Illustration 10

Scenario/Trigger

Z company, a medium sized entrepreneurial organisation, has recently been taken over by Q, a large international listed group. Within Z line managers had extensive responsibility for managing their departments whereas Q has dedicated HR professionals who work with line managers.

Specific concerns have been raised over how the roles of line managers with Z may be affected by the merger.

Task

Prepare a briefing document outlining the key areas where line manager roles within Z are likely to be redefined.

Suggested approach

- Note down the traditional differences between the roles of line managers and HR professionals.

- Go through the list and see which relate to the specific circumstances of Z (and Q).

- Prioritise the above points.

- I can discuss the roles of communication, negotiation, influence and persuasion in the management process

- I can negotiate with relevant stakeholders

- I can assist in effective decisions making within the organisation

- I can communicate effectively with relevant stakeholders

Illustration 11

Scenario/Trigger

B company will shortly close operations in one European country as it is moving manufacturing to Asia.

Task

Identify the stakeholder groups which need to be informed and discuss appropriate methods of communication for each group identified.

Suggested approach

- Brainstorm stakeholder groups.
- Decide which groups will have an interest in this decision.
- Consider possible communication methods e.g. email, letter, meeting.
- Based on importance and sensitivity of stakeholder, determine most appropriate communication method for each.

- I can discuss the use and limitations of relevant cash flows for decision making (P1)

Illustration 12

Scenario/Trigger

S company is assessing whether to agree to a proposal for a special "one-off" contract.

Task

Discuss whether or not the company should accept the proposal.

Suggested approach

- Consider the main techniques available – e.g. relevant cash flows is more useful for assessing a "one-off" contract.

- Link the advantages and disadvantages of these techniques to information given in the scenario – e.g. relevant cash flows will give a better indication of the impact of the contract on shareholder wealth but fails to incorporate non-financial aspects – for example, impact on the environment, treatment of workforce, etc.

- Consider any assumptions that have been made regarding future growth, prices, etc.

- Make clear recommendations if asked for.

- I can collaborate with managers, product owners and other relevant stakeholders

3.4 Leadership skills

At the operational level the skills within this generic competency fall within the E1 syllabus in terms of applied knowledge but in terms of coaching and mentoring skills could arise from any part of P1, E1 and F1. In some cases it could simply be that students are asked to make preliminary recommendations concerning an issue.

Here is a sample of the competencies which you may be expected to demonstrate:

- I can develop individuals by considering the issues associated with training, evaluation and progression

Illustration 13

Scenario/Trigger

C company offers a range of financial training products across several sites in a large European city. Some members of staff are based in one location all the time but most travel to each site to deliver training and support students. C has now organised staff into virtual teams with appointed line managers.

Task

Advise the line manager how effective training, evaluation and progression can motivate members of virtual teams, making recommendations.

Suggested approach

- Make a note of the pros/cons of virtual teams (E1).

- Try to put yourself in the situation of the team members – what would your concerns be? What factors might result in poor motivation?

- Consider how effective training, evaluation and progression can address these concerns.

- Make recommendations.

- I can advise on the wider implications of maintaining a quality brand once it is established (E1).

- I can advise on the appropriate course of action given an identified ethical dilemma (E1).

3.5 Integration marks

There are 3 marks for integration skills at the operational level. These may be incorporated into the mark allocations of any of the four categories above and can involve a mixture of the following:

- Being able to see the "bigger picture" and "wider context" relating to an issue – for example, the implications on the firm as a whole

- Linking discussions to each of the three underlying papers

- Linking discussions between the current and previous tasks in the exam

For example, in the examiner's reports we have had the following statements:

- "There were three marks available for integration of knowledge within each variant. Candidates who commented around a subject area and brought in other relevant information from other subject areas or syllabi were awarded these marks." (May 2015, Aug 2015)

- "There were three marks available for integration and those candidates who fully addressed the tasks in an appropriate manner will have scored these marks." (Nov 2015, Feb 2016)

You should now have a better understand of how the technical knowledge from previous studies may translate into what you need to be able to DO in the exam in the form of competencies. You should also now recognise if it is likely that you will have some gaps in your knowledge which you will need to revisit.

4 Summary

Next steps:

(1) You can begin to revisit and revise technical material from your previous studies according to the summaries given in this chapter. However we suggest you continue to do this alongside working through the rest of this book so you can also learn how you may need to apply the knowledge.

(2) Remember that you are unlikely to have to perform calculations in the case study exam. However you may need to explain or interpret calculations and so an appreciation of how they are prepared is still relevant and useful.

Integrating skills and knowledge

Chapter learning objectives

- To understand how the learning outcomes and skills derived from the individual papers are integrated within the case study competencies and tasks.

1 Triggers and tasks – integrating the skills

In the previous chapter we considered each competency in isolation. It is important that you understand how these competencies will be linked in the examination. We can now bring together these skills into a series of integrated tasks.

Consider the following short scenario:

Scenario – Company Z

Company Z manufactures a range of kitchen gadgets using advanced production line techniques in its South East Asian factory. Much of the process of manufacture is automated although reliable supervisors are required to monitor the machinery and minimise any downtime caused by faults.

The company ships the gadgets to a range of European ports and the goods are sold in high street household goods shops and also through several large online retailers.

Profits in Z have declined significantly in the past 12 months and the Board believes this may be due to uncompetitive pricing and has asked you, as the senior management accountant, to investigate.

This is an example of what CIMA refer to in the Case study exam as a **trigger**. This information and the events occurring will give rise to one or more tasks. These tasks are likely to come from a range of different generic competency areas.

Technical skills

So the first task you may be asked to complete could demonstrate your technical skills. One of the skills here is to

'Apply various costing methods such as standard, marginal and absorption methods and explain corresponding advantages and disadvantages.'

So you may be asked to do the following:

Task 1

Prepare a briefing note for the Board explaining the issues involved with the current absorption costing system and evaluate a suitable alternative.

Given the information in the trigger (and much more detailed company and environmental information provided in the pre-seen information) you are likely to conclude that a company such as Z should be using ABC to more effectively calculate full product costs and that this could have an impact on pricing.

Business skills

As part of the business skills competency you need to show that you can 'analyse the global business environment'. This may include recognising that other factors will affect pricing and you are given the opportunity to demonstrate this understanding in the next task:

Task 2

Evaluate the external factors that Z needs to take into account when setting suitable prices.

People skills

Another key generic competency that you will be required to demonstrate involves people skills such as the ability to 'influence relevant stakeholders'.

It is possible that you will be tested on your understanding of relevant theory and techniques explaining how to influence. However it is also likely that you will show your ability through actually influencing relevant stakeholders through the task.

So you could be asked to do the following:

Task 3

Write a report for the HR Director which discusses the impact on the organisation of the move towards ABC and evaluate how the changes can be managed.

Leadership skills

The final generic competency is leadership. It is interesting that there are 6% of the marks devoted to leadership skills but the table correlating generic case study competences to individual papers does not show anything for this category:

CIMA COMPETENCY FRAMEWORK

Competencies	Syllabus area		
Technical skills	E1	P1	F1
Financial accounting and reporting			F1
Cost accounting and management		P1	
Planning and control		P1	
Management reporting and analysis		P1	
Corporate finance and treasury management			
Risk management and internal control		P1	
Taxation		P1	F1
Accounting information systems	E1	P1	F1
Business skills			
Strategy			
Market environment	E1		
Process management	E1		
Business relations	E1		
Project management			
Regulatory environment			F1
Macro-economic anlaysis			
People skills			
Influence			
Negotiation			
Decision making		P1	
Communication	E1		
Collaboration and partnering	E1		
Leadership skills			
Team building			
Coaching and mentoring			
Driving performance			
Motivating and inspiring			
Change management			
Underpinned by ethics, integrity and professionalism			

This is partly because your role is that of a finance officer rather than manager. However, you could still be asked to advise a manager of how to implement strategies through, say, being asked to draft a statement to employees to "motivate and inspire staff". Alternatively you might be asked to "act in a coaching and mentoring fashion with respect to giving feedback on work already completed by someone else".

So you may be required to complete the following task:

Task 4

Write a letter to the employees of Z explaining the move towards an ABC system, clearly showing the reasons for the move and the likely impact it will have on the staff and the organisation.

So to summarise the progression here:

> Prepare a briefing note for the Board explaining the issues involved with the current absorption costing system and evaluate a suitable alternative.

Do accounting and finance work

> Write a report for the Board which sets out your advice on the appropriate basis for pricing at Z. Your report should include an evaluation of the external factors which Z needs to take into account when setting suitable process.

In the context of the business

> Discuss the impact on the organisation of moving towards an ABC system and evaluate how such a change can be managed.

To influence people

> Write a letter to the employees of Z explaining the move towards an ABC system, clearly showing the reasons for the move and the likely impact it will have on the staff and the organisation.

And lead within the organisation

2 Triggers and tasks – integrating the technical syllabi

As well as integrating the competencies it is useful to understand how the different technical papers on which the case study builds (E1, P1 and F1) are integrated in the exam.

The above series of tasks can be mapped out as follows:

	P1	E1	F1
Technical skills	(1) Explain the issues involved with the current absorption costing system and evaluate a suitable alternative.		
Business skills		(2) Evaluate the external factors which Z needs to take into account when deciding a marketing plan.	
People skills		(3) Discuss the impact on the organisation of moving towards an ABC system and advise how such a change may be managed.	

Leadership skills		(4) Explain the move towards an ABC system to the employees, clearly showing the reasons for the move and the likely impact it will have on the staff and the organisation	

As you can see this series of tasks does not contain any skills from F1 in this instance. The exam weightings for the case study are based on the competencies rather than the syllabi. However, across the whole case study you should always expect a balance of P1, E1 and F1.

Let's look at another scenario:

Company P manufactures a variety of high quality white electrical goods. Many of these use a specialised control component supplied by Company Q.

In recent bad weather one of Q's factories experienced severe flooding resulting in Q not being able to supply P with its required number of components for the next two months. Company P has been unable to find an alternative source of supply.

A similar series of tasks to the first example, incorporating a different range of technical content, could be mapped as follows:

	P1	E1	F1
Technical skills	(1) You have performed key factor analysis (supplied) to prioritise which products should be made to make the best use of the scarce components. You are then asked to advise the production manager using the results of your analysis and any other factors you feel should be considered.		(4) If production is brought in house, then various assets will have to be purchased. You are asked to explain the impact on the financial statements of a number of specific aspects.

Business skills		(2) The production manager has suggested bringing component manufacture in-house and you are asked to discuss the pros and cons of outsourcing compared with having production in-house.	
People skills		(3) Discuss techniques which can be used in recruiting suitable staff for the new production.	
Leadership skills		(4) Discuss techniques which can be used in recruiting suitable staff for the new production.	

3 Summary

You should now appreciate how the different technical areas from previous studies may integrate and form more complex triggers and tasks. You should also understand how you may see progression through the four generic competency areas.

Next steps:

(1) Return to the previous chapter and consider the range of competency statements which we gave you. Can you create your own integrated tasks using skills from each of the technical syllabi?

(2) Think about your own role at work. Where do you use technical skills? What about Business skills? Do you have much opportunity to use People skills or even Leadership? Thinking about your own experiences is very useful in generating ideas in the exam.

Pilot exam – preseen information

Chapter learning objectives

1 Introduction

The Case Study Examinations are like no other CIMA exam; there is no new syllabus to study or formulae to learn. The best way to be successful at this level is to practise using past case study exams and mock exams based on your real live case study. By reviewing previous case studies alongside your current case you will improve your commercial thought processes and will be more aware of what the examiner expects. By sitting mock exams, under timed conditions you can hone your exam techniques and, in particular, your time management skills.

This textbook is therefore based on this principle. It presents the pilot case study and uses this to demonstrate the skills and techniques that you must master to be successful. The first pilot case, MW, will be used to walkthrough the processes and approach. The remainder of this chapter contains the MW pre-seen material.

We would advise that you skim read this now before moving on to Chapter 5 where you will be provided with more guidance on how to familiarise yourself with the pre-seen material.

2 Reference material 1

General background:

MW is a manufacturer of animal feed in the form of dry food pellets for farm animals. It has established a reputation for producing quality products which are often recommended by vets and farmers because of their high nutritional quality. Currently MW manufactures food pellets for chicken and sheep.

MW is a family owned business, based in the UK, operating from a small rented factory and warehouse. Mr Harris the founder of MW developed the chicken and sheep food pellets six years ago when he was made redundant from his position as a product developer in a major animal feed manufacturer. Since developing these products he has spent his time building up MW's customer base and until recently had not really focused on developing any new products or enhancing the existing products.

Sales and customer history:

Six years ago Mr Harris started selling the food pellets to local farmers within a 20 kilometre radius of the factory. These farmers often took the pellets on an initial free trial with 90% of them coming back to place orders. Within a year MW was selling to farmers within a 100 kilometre radius from the factory as a result of word of mouth recommendations within the local farming community.

Four years ago sales were boosted when a local vet, who wrote articles for the weekly publication for vets, known as Vet Weekly, wrote an article praising the nutritional quality of MW's food pellets (this article is shown in reference material 2). A year after the article appeared sales had increased by 200% with MW generating revenues of nearly £4,000,000 in the year to 31 December 2012. MW now sells to farmers across the country and also to one major farm animal feed distributor, under a contract which was secured two months after the article was published.

Purchases and supplier information:

MW currently manufactures just two products, chicken and sheep food pellets, which are known within the business as CHICKEN and SHEEP. Both products are sold in standard sized bags. CHICKEN is sold in 15 kilogram bags and SHEEP in 30 kilogram bags. The recipes for CHICKEN and SHEEP have been unchanged for the last six years.

Both products require different combinations of two key ingredient mixes, which are known as ingredient R and ingredient S. Both of these ingredients are sourced from just one supplier, BF, which is also located in the UK. MW has always purchased its ingredients from BF and there has always been a good working relationship between the two companies. Up until a month ago BF was a family run business, however it has recently been taken over by a large multi-national company, although it still operates under the name of BF.

Accounting and costing systems used by MW:

Due to the simplicity of the business (that is, the manufacture of only two products and only one supplier) the accounting systems used by MW are very basic. Business transactions are recorded on a standard accounting software package within the factory office by the accountant. The financial statements are prepared annually by an external firm of accountants. In the UK, MW is exempt from an annual audit.

Currently the business does not prepare an annual budget. However standard cost cards are produced for each product at the start of each financial year to give Mr Harris an approximation of the cost of a bag of each product to enable him to determine selling prices. The latest standard cost cards established on 1 October 2014 and the basis of their preparation are included for reference (see reference material 3).

Current market conditions and new Research and Development facility:

Over the last two years the market has become much more competitive, with other larger companies investing heavily in the production of nutritional animal feed. As a result Mr Harris has recently established a research and development facility to develop new and improved products. His daughter Zoe who has just successfully qualified as a biochemist, but has not previously been involved in the business, will work in the facility. The local newspaper recently published a feature on this development (see reference material 4).

MW results and position:

MW's latest financial statements for the year to 30 September 2014 are attached for reference (see reference material 5).

The business has maintained a good level of profitability and as a result been able to pay a significant level of dividend to Mr Harris, as well as, cash levels having been built up. MW has never taken out any form of external debt as the set up was funded from Mr Harris's redundancy monies which were initially loaned to the company through a director's loan account but which have all now been repaid. Mr Harris does have a close relationship with his bank manager however and believes that if required he would be able to secure external bank finance.

MW's employees:

Mr Harris and his wife are the only directors and MW currently employs a further 26 people in the business. This is broken down as follows:

Production	16
Distribution	6
Research and development	1
Factory office	3

The three people employed in the office are:

- Mr Webb – the production and distribution manager

- Miss Lyons – the sales manager (part time)

- Yourself – the accountant (you have been with MW for only 1 month)

3 Reference material 2 – Article (Vet Weekly)

Blended feed success

1 August 2011   Article Author: James Perkins

MW blended animal feed is proving to be very successful with farmers in our area, providing supplements to produce high quality forage for both sheep and chickens. The secret, or not really a secret lies in the highly accurate pre-formulated mix of ingredients, which achieve an effective nutritional balance, taking the guesswork out of mixing the ingredients with forage on the farm. It is well known that minerals and vitamins are an essential component of all animal diets, however bad formulation and in-balances in mineral nutrition can result in major health problems for the animals.

Problems can also result from either too high or too low a level of minerals, many forage diets being low in minerals in any event. This manifests itself in reduced immune function, leading to disease susceptibility and poor quality animals. Excess minerals can be toxic, with the inevitable consequences for the animals, increased environmental pollution, and also wastes money.

Farmers know that easily digestible energy and protein is particularly important for sheep, particularly females during pregnancy. MW's 'SHEEP' feed is readily digested with a good fibre level and sugar balance, eliminating the problem of the excess fibre levels in some feeds which can reduce nutrition intake and prevent effective digestion.

Magnesium and potassium levels are also important, the effective blending of these in a molasses mix ensures that they are digested and absorbed rapidly and the correct balance achieved.

The sheep find this very palatable (tasty) when mixed with other lower quality forage, which may otherwise be unusable, and water. It is being proven that continual feeding of this blend is both cost effective and has the added benefit of assisting in eliminating 'twin lamb disease', high lamb loss, small weak lambs and 'the staggers.'

Similar observations can be made with 'CHICKEN'. Modern hybrid hens require a well-balanced nutritional feed ensuring a consistent feeding regime at each stage of their development, in order to ensure consistently high internal and external egg quality. The formulation of 'CHICKEN' is enabling this to be achieved, with hens each producing over 300 eggs a year.

The success of 'CHICKEN' is that it is produced with the correct balance of highly digestible materials containing a precise mix of dietary fibre and sugars which contain the natural antioxidants and essential oils required for a healthy bird.

Further benefits of this well balanced feed include assisting in promoting sound skeletal development, good feather quality, efficient growth at all stages, and help to build the natural immune systems of the birds.

It is in this way that MW's 'CHICKEN' and 'SHEEP' are proving themselves in our local farming community and seem set for an increasingly successful future with hopefully a broadening of the product range and continuing product developments.

4 Reference material 3 – Standard Cost Cards

MW
Standard cost cards
1 October 2014

Chicken

Per bag of production	Quantity	Price/rate	Total cost £
Ingredient R	11kg	£0.35 per kg	3.85
Ingredient S	9kg	£0.25 per kg	2.25
Direct labour	9 mins	£10 per hour	1.50
Variable overhead	9 mins	£6 per direct labour hour	0.90
Fixed overhead	9 mins	£38.75 per direct labour hour	5.81
Total expected cost per bag			**14.31**

Sheep

Per bag of production	Quantity	Price/rate	Total cost £
Ingredient R	3kg	£0.35 per kg	1.05
Ingredient S	35kg	£0.25 per kg	8.75
Direct labour	12 mins	£10 per hour	2.00
Variable overhead	12 mins	£6 per direct labour hour	1.20
Fixed overhead	12 mins	£38.75 per direct labour hour	7.75
Total expected cost per bag			**20.75**

Labour hours calculations:

	CHICKEN	SHEEP
Direct labour time for a bag of product	9 mins	12 mins
Total expected production	60,000 bags	75,000 bags
Therefore, total expected direct labour hours	9,000 hrs	15,000 hrs

Fixed overhead rate per hour:

Expected annual fixed overhead costs for the year are £930,000 and total direct labour hours are 24,000. Therefore, the fixed overhead rate is £38.75 per direct labour hour.

Notes:

- The time for a bag of production was measured in 2012.
- Expected production is based upon the best estimate of sales for the year to 30 September 2015.
- The variable overhead rate of £6 per hour was established in 2012.
- Fixed overheads of £930,000 are based upon that expected for last year with a 2% increase.

5 Reference material 4 – Newspaper Article

Retail News

20th May 2014 | No 7893   Retail Paper of the Year | £2.50

MW goes from strength to strength

Local animal feed company MW has been doing well recently. In an interview with our farming correspondent, Mark Harris, the founder and owner of MW, says he is pleased with developments to date.

Mark invested all his redundancy money into the business when he left one of the large multinational owned feed companies and admits 'it was a daunting prospect, starting a business from nothing, but I decided it was too early to retire. I felt my technical skills in the animal food industry could be put to good use, so invested all my payoff in the business.'

He admits to some misgivings at the time, 'competing with the large multinationals was always going to be tough, but I felt there was a gap in the market which someone with local farming knowledge and the right technical skills could fill. The larger producers can become too remote from their markets sometimes, inflexible and always relying on their proprietary products to sell well.'

It seems Mark has achieved his early ambitions, 'being close to the market, our local farmers, listening to their problems and requirements, combined with the technical skills and flexibility of a small producer have been key', he says. 'As a result we have been able to offer effective solutions, building trust in our products, developing good relationships with the local farming community.'

MW has grown to the stage where it now employs 26 people, but what of the future? 'More of the same I hope' says Mark, 'with our existing rather limited range selling well, we need to increase our ability to serve this market, and also given the success of our strategy, expand our production facilities and broaden our product range. I'm sure if we stick to our current skills and don't lose our links with our local market we will succeed.'

Mark reveals his plans for the business involve moving to better, larger facilities, improving the technical research abilities and also an expansion in the workforce.

'But this is all for the future, we will have to see how things develop', he says.

It seems that from small beginnings and with his technical and entrepreneurial skills Mark will be steering the business to greater things over the next few years, providing valuable benefits to the farming and local communities, the future looks good for MW.

6 Reference material 5 – Financial Statements

MW Statement of Profit or Loss for MW for the year ended 30 September:		
	2014 £	2013 £
Revenue	4,211,000	4,050,000
Cost of sales	(2,400,000)	(2,300,000)
Gross profit	1,811,000	1,750,000
Administrative expenses	(860,000)	(835,000)
Distribution costs	(85,000)	(80,000)
Profit before tax	866,000	835,000
Tax	(217,000)	(209,000)
Profit for the year	649,000	626,000

	Note	2014 £	2014 £	2013 £	2013 £
MW Statement of Financial Position of MW as at 30 September					
ASSETS					
Non-current assets					
Plant and equipment	1	80,000		100,000	
			80,000		100,000
Current assets					
Inventories	2	198,000		180,000	
Trade and other receivables		580,000		510,000	
Cash and cash equivalents		952,100		724,100	
			1,730,100		1,414,100
Total assets			**1,810,100**		**1,514,100**
EQUITY AND LIABILITIES					
Ordinary share capital issued		100		100	
Retained earnings		1,333,000		1,065,000	
Total equity			1,333,100		1,065,100
Current liabilities					
Trade and other payables		260,000		240,000	
Tax payable	3	217,000		209,000	
			477,000		449,000
Total equity and liabilities			**1,810,100**		**1,514,100**

Notes

(1) Plant and equipment are stated after charging depreciation.

(2) Inventories consist of both raw materials and finished goods.

(3) The corporate income tax rate is 25%.

MW Statement of Changes in Equity for MW for the year ended 30 September 2014	Share capital	Share premium	Retained earnings	Total
	£	£	£	£
Balance at 1 January 2014	100	–	1,065,000	1,065,100
Profit for the year	–	–	649,000	649,000
Dividends paid	–	–	(381,000)	(381,000)
Balance at 31 December 2014	**100**	–	**1,333,000**	**1,333,100**

MW		
Statement of Cash Flows for MW for the year ended 30 September 2014		
	£	£
Cash flows from operating activities		
Profit before tax	866,000	
Adjustments		
Depreciation	20,000	
	———	
	886,000	
Movements in working capital		
Increase in inventories	(18,000)	
Increase in trade receivables	(70,000)	
Increase in trade payables	20,000	
	———	
Cash generated from operations	818,000	
Tax paid	(209,000)	
	———	
Net cash from operating activities		609,000
Cash flows from financing activities		
Dividend paid	(381,000)	
	———	
Net cash from financing activities		(381,000)
		———
Net increase in cash and cash equivalents		228,000
Cash and cash equivalents at the beginning of the year		724,100
		———
Cash and cash equivalents at the end of the year		**952,100**
		———

7 Reference material 6 – Industry Report

THE ASSOCIATION OF ANIMAL FEED

INDUSTRY REPORT FOR 2014 AND BEYOND

Introductory Message from the Chief Executive:

Welcome to this, the 20th annual report from The Association of Animal Feed Producers in the UK.

As you will see from the statistics and analysis presented in this report, 2014 has been a positive year for the industry both globally and in the UK. Global production of animal feed is fast approaching the 1 billion tonne mark as the ever expanding population fuels growth in the meat and animal products industry. Indeed with the global population set to reach 9 billion by 2050, this growth and expansion can only increase.

Within the UK animal feed production has now reached approximately 1.2% of total global production which is a slight increase from the previous year at 1.1%. The industry is thriving, especially for niche products from the small but growing independent sector.

There are challenges ahead, however all the signs are that 2015 and beyond will show increased growth and opportunity.

Terry Jones
Chief Executive

Global production statistics for 2014:

Production of farm animal feed throughout the world in 2014 has been as follows:

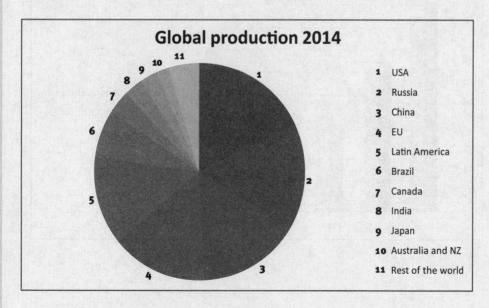

Global production 2014

1 USA
2 Russia
3 China
4 EU
5 Latin America
6 Brazil
7 Canada
8 India
9 Japan
10 Australia and NZ
11 Rest of the world

	Tonnes (million)	%
USA	168	17.7
Russia	154	16.2
China	144	15.2
EU*	141	14.8
Latin America (excluding Brazil)	125	13.2
Brazil	68	7.2
Canada	33	3.5
India	28	2.9
Japan	26	2.7
Australia and New Zealand	18	1.9
Rest of the world	45	4.7
Total	**950**	

*this includes 11 million tonnes for production from the UK.

UK industry statistics:

Production by animal type for 2014 and 2013 is shown in the following graph:

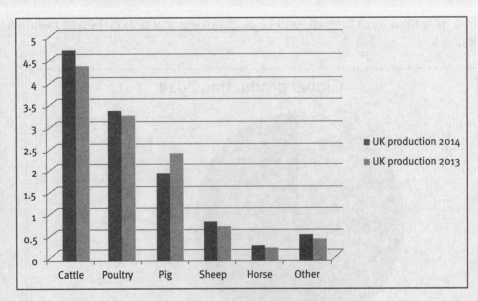

	Tonnes (thousands) 2014	Tonnes (thousands) 2013
Cattle feed	4,610	4,253
Poultry feed	3,254	3,140
Pig feed	1,840	2,300
Sheep feed	765	620
Horse feed	215	182
Other feeds*	450	361
	11,134	10,856

*other feeds includes goats and llamas

Composition of UK producers:

	*Small scale producers % of total production	National producers % of total production
Cattle feed	15.2	84.8
Poultry feed	25.1	74.9
Pig feed	33.0	67.0
Sheep feed	58.4	41.6
Horse feed	65.1	34.9
Other feeds*	70.3	29.7

* small scale is defined as a UK producer with revenue of less than £10 million a year

UK industry analysis:

The industry in the UK has followed the EU trend with output increasing by approximately 2.6% from 2013. Total EU production in 2014 was 141 million tonnes, around 15 % of the global output, of which the UK production accounts for 11 million tonnes or 8% of EU and 1.2% of global output. In the UK slight decreases in the overall production of pig feed have been offset by increases in cattle and poultry feed, which remain the leading segments of compound feed production.

The most important factors in the feed demand have been the gradual economic recovery, which has led to an increasing trend in the cost of feed production materials. With regard to ruminants the severe wet weather of late winter and early spring have led to lower forage harvests, but the good autumnal weather conditions have favoured grass growth and helped restore some stability. Within the EU there are big differences between member countries with the Czech Republic and Denmark showing declines of 14% and 7% respectively, but with Germany and Poland achieving positive growth of around 3%, mainly due to increasing exports. As a result Germany maintains its position as the leading producer of compound feeds, with France and Spain in second and third position respectively.

Key drivers in the compound feed market have been new standards for the cages for laying hens and new group housing requirements for pig production. The unfortunate development of the Schmallenberg virus in ruminant populations has also had an adverse effect on demand.

On the feed ingredients side, high prices for all feed materials both energy sources like cereals and protein sources like soya bean meal have resulted from continued high Chinese demand. Seasonal drought in South America has also added to high material costs and will continue to affect industry profitability.

As a consequence of these factors it is expected that cattle and poultry feed production will increase slightly by 1%, and pig feed reduce by 0.5%, giving an overall stable level of compound feed production for next year.

Challenges and opportunities facing the UK animal feed industry:

As noted in the overall market analysis in the previous section the UK forms a small but increasingly influential segment of the overall market. Feed producers in the UK have become increasingly successful at producing nutritional feed. This is particularly important as a move away from the use of antibiotics to control disease is taking place. As in humans the continued use of such drugs is proving increasingly ineffective at dealing with some diseases, and is ultimately having a detrimental effect on the quality of livestock.

As a result feed manufacturers have become increasingly reliant on amino acids and enzymes to boost quality and prevent diseases in livestock. The global market for such additives was valued at $16,183 million in 2012 and was estimated to have risen 25% to $20,233 million last year, further increasing producer price pressures, and driving the search for innovative and cost effective compounds.

The process is supported and encouraged by the European Platform for the Responsible Use of Medicines in Animals (EPRUMA), a multi stakeholder platform supported by the feed industry, livestock farmers, veterinarians, the animal health industry and other key partners of the livestock chain and of the pet world. This promotes regimes which ensure adequate animal nutrition, meeting both the physiological and physical feed structure requirements which are a prerequisite to maintaining the health of farm animals.

The import of other essential ingredients forms another important part in the overall development of the industry. Maintaining a reliable supply of one of the main ingredients, soya, along with palm oil and palm kernel oil, (20% of all palm oil and 83% of all palm kernel oil imported into the UK is used in producing animal feed), is increasingly important. As such the industry is increasingly looking to protect the sustainability of supplies and acting in partnership with producers. The industry participates in the Round Table on Responsible Soy (RTRS) which in 2010 developed and adopted the first global standard for responsible soya production.

This is the result of a multi-stakeholder negotiation and bans the use of certain agrochemicals and also lays down standards for responsible labour conditions, community relations, environmental responsibility as well as legal compliance and good business practice in the growing regions.

Energy use is another increasing challenge for the industry. It is estimated that energy consumption of the 130 UK production sites is running at 2 terawatt hours a year, generating carbon emissions of 620,000 tonnes, and as a result the increasing use of technology to control and reduce this is of increasing importance.

These factors, together with changing weather patterns, disease outbreaks and global supply and demand fluctuations together with an ever increasing global population combine to present an increasingly challenging environment for the industry.

8 Summary

We are now working through the Pilot exam from beginning to end so you can see all of the skills and techniques which may be required in this exam. This chapter simply reproduces the pre-seen information for the Pilot exam and we will work through this in more detail in the next two chapters.

Next steps:

(1) Make sure you have at least skim read the pre-seen before moving on to Chapter Five where we will consider how to do further analysis.

(2) It might be useful to make a list at this point of what you think some of the relevant technical areas might be – are you comfortable with these areas?

5

Pilot exam – analysing the preseen

Chapter learning objectives

- to understand various techniques and models that can help familiarisation with the pre-seen.
- tax regime

1 The importance of familiarisation

The pre-seen material is released approximately seven weeks before you sit the exam and one of your first tasks will be to analyse the context within which the case is set. Although your responses in the exam will be driven by the unseen material, you will only be able to fully assess the impact of each event on the organisation if you have a sufficient depth of knowledge and awareness of both the organisation and the industry in which it operates.

The purpose of the pre-seen material is to allow you to gain that knowledge and awareness. Remember, you will be acting in the position of a management accountant who works for the organisation in a finance officer role. It will therefore be expected that you will have the same level of familiarisation as someone fulfilling that role.

It is extremely important that you study the pre-seen material thoroughly before you go into the examination. There are two main reasons for this:

- It will save time in the examination itself if you are already familiar with the pre-seen material (especially in relation to how any costing information is presented).

- It enables you to develop a view of the situation facing the organisation in the case study.

You will not be able to respond to the examination tasks from the pre-seen material alone; the unseen material given to you in the examination will present significant new information that may alter the situation substantially. Even so, a major step towards success in the examination is a careful study, exploration and understanding of the pre-seen material.

Each set of pre-seen material is different but as a general rule, you can expect the following:

- Industry background

- History of the business

- Key personnel

- Current business/industry issues

- Management accounting information, such as costing schedules

- Financial Statements

- Tax regime

Each of these areas will need reviewing in detail.

You should question what each piece of information tells you, and why the examiner may have given it to you.

2 Exhibit by exhibit analysis

The purpose of this initial stage is to lay a foundation for further analysis. It's more about asking questions than finding solutions. Before you do anything else, you should read the pre-seen material from beginning to end without making any notes, simply to familiarise yourself with the scenario.

Read the material again, as many times as you think necessary, without making notes. You can do this over a period of several days, if you wish.

When you think you are reasonably familiar with the situation described by the material, you should start to make notes. By making notes, you will become more familiar with the detail of the scenario.

- Try to make notes on each paragraph (or each group of short paragraphs) in the pre-seen material.

- Think about what the paragraph is telling you, and consider why this information might be of interest or relevance.

- Ask yourself "why might the examiner have told me this?".

- Try to make your questions as broad as possible; consider as many different stakeholders as possible and try to put yourself in different positions (say the CEO, a key customer, a franchise operator etc.) to consider the information from different perspectives.

Illustration 1 – MW: Introductory overview

Given below is an example of some questions you could ask yourself relating to the first exhibit of the Operational case Study pilot exam pre-seen information.

Question	Potential response
What factors may have limited growth for MW to date?	• MW produces animal feed, which is likely to be bulky to ship. This is why the radius for customers began as only 20 kilometres. • The company has also largely relied on reputation and word of mouth to increase awareness and this will have limitations in terms of the amount of growth which can be expected. • The market has also experienced increases in levels of competition which can make growth difficult for a smaller company. • Reliance on 1 supplier for the 2 key ingredients has possibly constrained growth.

Comment on financing at MW.	• Currently MW has no debt, which means there is less risk should the company suffer any cash flow problems, as no interest payments are required. This has also ensured that cash has been available to pay out dividends.
	• This lack of debt finance may limit the potential for long term growth.
	• MW has a good relationship with the bank and so a loan may be possible. The company should consider the terms they would be willing to accept and if they have assets to use as security.
Why might MW consider preparing budgets in the future?	• To show the bank or other potential future investors what plans the company has.
	• To assist in planning the required levels of resource such as future staffing.
	• To assess whether additional finance may be required in the future.
Are there any specific new developments mentioned?"	• R&D department established – will need to account for these costs in the financial statements.

3 Note taking

When you're making notes, try to be as creative as possible. Psychologists tell us that using conventional linear notes on their own use only a small part of our mental capacity. They are hard to remember and prevent us from drawing connections between topics. This is because they seek to classify things under hierarchical headings.

Here are some techniques that candidates find useful. See which ones work for you as you practise on the pilot case in this text.

Spider diagrams

Spider diagrams (or clustering diagrams) are a quick graphic way of summarising connections between subjects.

You cannot put much detail into a spider diagram, just a few key words. However, it does help you to 'visualise' the information in the case material.

You must expect to update your spider diagram as you go along and to redraft it when it starts to get too messy. It is all part of the learning process.

Timelines

Timelines are valuable to make sense of the sequence of events in the pre-seen and to understand where the company in the case study presently stands. The case study exam takes place in real time, so you need to be clear how long is likely to elapse between the data in the pre-seen and the actual exam. This is the time period during which the issues facing the company can be incorporated into the unseen material.

The case writer is not trying to trick you or spring something entirely unexpected on you, but you need to be aware of the timeframe and the changes that have already occurred in the company's history, so that you can offer realistic advice for the company's future.

Organisation charts

Preparing an organisation chart will familiarise you with the roles and the overlaps, and also help you to identify gaps or ambiguities in roles, as well as helping you to remember the names and roles of the key people in the case. In some cases this will be provided for you; where it isn't, you may want to draw one out.

Post-it-notes

Post-it-notes can be used to stick onto each page of the printed pre-seen material and to jot key points on. Additionally, you may want to keep a post-it-note for each person, and as you work through the pre-seen material. You could even stick the notes on your desk, a notice board or wall so that you can keep glancing at them to remember who's who in the case and what issues and problems have been identified. You could also jot down your ideas for alternative directions that the company could take, to prepare you for exam day.

Colours

Colours help you remember things you may want to draw upon in the exam room. You could write down all your financial calculations and observations in green whilst having red for organisational and blue for strategic. Some candidates use different colour highlighter pens to emphasise different aspects of the pre-seen material perhaps using the same colour coding suggestion.

Additionally, sometimes making notes in different colours helps you to remember key facts and some of the preparation that you have done using the pre-seen material.

Use whatever colours work for you – but it does help to make notes on both the pre-seen material and the research you do. DO NOT just read the material – you must take notes (in whatever format) and if colours help you to understand and link your research together then use colours.

4 Technical analysis

Now you're reasonably familiar with the material it's time to carry out some technical analysis to help you identify and understand the issues facing the company.

A good starting point is to revise any 'technical' topics that might be relevant. The pre-seen material might make a reference to a particular 'technical' issue, such as TQM, ABC, CSR, the marketing mix, big data, HRM, and so on.

If you lack confidence on any topic that might be relevant, go back to your previous study materials and revise it if necessary.

5 Financial analysis

You will almost certainly be given some figures in the pre-seen material. These might relate to the company's profits or losses, or product profitability. There might be statements of profit or loss and statements of financial position for previous years, future business plans, cash flow statements, capital expenditure plans, and so on.

A key part of your initial analysis will be to perform some simple financial analysis, such as financial ratio calculations or a cash flow analysis. These might give you a picture of changes in profitability, liquidity, working capital management or cash flows over time, and will help ensure you have a rounded picture of the organisation's current position.

If a cash flow statement is not provided, it may be worth preparing a summary of cash flows. You may have to make some assumptions if the detailed information isn't provided but even with these, there is great value in appreciating where the money has come from, and where it is being spent.

Profitability ratios

You might find useful information from an analysis of profit/sales ratios, for:

* the company as a whole
* each division, or
* each product or service.

Profit margins can be measured as a net profit percentage and as a gross profit percentage. You can then look at trends in the ratios over time, or consider whether the margins are good or disappointing.

Analysing the ratio of certain expenses to sales might also be useful, such as the ratio of administration costs to sales, sales and marketing costs to sales or R&D costs to sales. Have there been any noticeable changes in these ratios over time and, if so, is it clear why the changes have happened?

Working capital ratios

Working capital ratios can be calculated to assess the efficiency of working capital management (= management of inventory, trade receivables and trade payables). They can also be useful for assessing liquidity, because excessive investment in working capital ties up cash and slows the receipt of cash.

The main working capital ratios are:

- "inventory days" or the average inventory holding period: a long period might indicate poor inventory management

- "receivable days" or the average time that customers take to pay: a long period could indicate issues with the collection of cash, although would need to consider this in light of the entity's credit terms and industry averages

- "payable days" or the average time to pay suppliers: a long period could indicate cash flow difficulties for the entity, although would need to consider in light of credit terms.

You should be familiar with these ratios and how to calculate the length of the cash cycle or operating cycle.

Cash flow analysis or funding analysis

If the main objective of a company is to maximise the wealth of its shareholders, the most important financial issues will be profitability and returns to shareholders. However, other significant issues in financial strategy are often:

- cash flows and liquidity, and

- funding

A possible cash flow problem occurs whenever the cash flows from operations do not appear to be sufficient to cover all the non-operational cash payments that the company has to make, such as spending on capital expenditure items.

An analysis of future funding can be carried out by looking at the history of changes in the statement of financial position. It is a relatively simple task to look at the growth in the company's assets over time, and at how the asset growth has been funded – by equity, long-term debt or shorter-term liabilities. If equity has funded much of the growth in assets, it might be possible to see how much of the new equity has been provided by retained profits, and how much has come from new issues of shares (indicated by an increase in the allotted share capital and share premium reserve).

Recap of key ratio calculations

Key ratios:

Ratio	Formula
Gross profit margin (GPM)	(Gross profit/Revenue) × 100%
Net profit margin (NPM)	(Net profit/Revenue) × 100%
Operating profit margin	(Operating profit/Revenue) × 100%
Profit before tax margin	(Profit before tax/Revenue) × 100%
Return on Capital Employed (ROCE)	(Operating profit/Capital employed) × 100%
Asset turnover	Revenue/Capital employed
Receivables days	(Trade receivables/Credit sales) × 365 days
Inventory days	(Inventory/Cost of sales) × 365 days
Payables days	(Trade Payables/Cost of sales) × 365 days

Exercise 1 – Basic Financial Analysis

Complete the following table using the information in Chapter four. Commentary on the results can be found in Chapter six.

Ratio	2014	*Working*	2013	*Working*
Revenue growth				
Operating profit margin				
Receivables days				
Payables days				
Inventory days				

6 Industry analysis and research

Why is industry research important?

Remember, part of your preparatory work is to analyse the context within which the case is set. A full analysis is not possible without an understanding of the industry and research may support the information provided in the pre-seen. From this analysis, you may be better able to understand the key issues and address the requirements.

The pre-seen material usually contains a good summary of relevant information about the industry. This can be relied on as accurate at the time it is published and will form the basis of your analysis. At the operational level the scope of this industry information will be relatively limited to reflect the fact that at this level many of the issues arising will have an internal organisational focus rather than an external one. In contrast, at strategic level the industry data provided with the pre-seen will be more detailed and varied to support analysis of the business from a strategic perspective.

You could further research the industry setting for the case you are working on so that you can develop a better understanding of the problems (and opportunities) facing companies in this industry. Hopefully, it will also stop you from making unrealistic comments in your answer on the day of the exam.

Industry research will allow you to add further comments in terms of:

- identifying potential problems currently facing the industry

- identifying the nature of competition and the basis for customer and supplier relationships

- considering the competitive strategies being followed by companies operating in the real world and how they are achieved (e.g. special technologies, use of brands) and whether they could be adopted by the company in the pre-seen

- identifying issues with operational aspects of real world firms.

Don't think that your preparation should be limited to just looking at the industry. A wider understanding of the way business is conducted and the influence of the economic and political environments on business could be just as useful.

How to conduct industry research

Remember that at operational level you will not be expected to undertake vast amounts of your own research into the industry. Having said that, such research will help you to more fully understand some of the issues affecting the organisation and to put yourself in the shoes of the person that you will need to be in the exam room. Therefore this section will give you some ideas and tools to help with this research.

Your research could incorporate any of the following sources of information:

- *Personal networks*

  If you happen to work in the industry described, then you could talk to colleagues about the case. If not, then perhaps family or friends with relevant experience could help.

- *News and Trade media*

  One of the best ways to achieve a wider appreciation of different industries and the economy in general is to regularly read the business pages of a good national newspaper. Some quality business newspapers may also carry special supplements on particular industries from time to time.

  If you can find trade journals, then these will obviously have more specific industry-related content.

- *Using the Internet*

  This is the most convenient and commonly used method of researching the industry, but as noted above, try to target the information you're looking for in order to avoid wasting time. Generally, you will be looking for the following sorts of information:

  – Websites of firms similar to the one(s) in the pre-seen material. This can help you learn about the sorts of products and competitive strategies they follow and may also yield financial information that can be compared with the data in the pre-seen material.

  – Trade journals of the industry in the pre-seen. This will provide information on real world environmental issues facing the business.

  – Articles on the industry in journals and newspapers. These will keep you up to date on developments.

  – Financial statements of real firms.

Further details are given below.

Further details on industry research

How to conduct industry research

One of the big problems with conducting industry research is thus knowing where to stop. In today's technology driven society, a wealth of information is available at your fingertips so perhaps the most important aspect when performing research is to focus on reliable sources.

In order to help direct your research, think about the following sources of information:

Personal networks

Some candidates have been lucky enough to find themselves facing a set of pre seen material describing the industry they work in. In this situation, they have plenty of colleagues they can talk to about the case.

Alternatively, and depending on the industry in the Case Study, it is possible that you know someone in the business from whom you can get information. Likely contacts include:

- people who work in the industry or who have worked in it

- family members or their friends

- contacts at work who have dealings with the industry in the case

- other people sitting the case study exam, either via your tuition provider or using online forums, such as CIMAsphere.

Discussing the case and your analysis of the situation of the business with an expert will help you to test out your understanding of what is important.

Trade media and news media

A journalist is a paid professional who searches out and presents information about an industry. If you can find a trade journal for the industry in the case, it will save you a lot of searching for yourself.

Trade journals can be located in three ways:

- Visit a good newsagent. The difficulty here is that only very large industries such as accounting, financial advising, computing, music and construction provide enough customers for a newsagent to consider stocking the magazine.

- Ask someone who works in the industry for the name of the journals for the industry.

- Use the Internet. Many trade journals now have websites and, in many cases, the journals can be downloaded as PDFs. Naturally there will be restrictions on logging in if you have not paid a fee, but there is a surprising amount of free media available. The best approach is to go to a search engine and type in a search inquiry such as: 'trade magazine for [name of industry] industry' or 'articles on [name of industry or real world firm]'.

News media is more general although some quality business newspapers may carry special supplements on particular industries from time to time.

It is also very important to spend time reading the financial pages of any good newspaper, not necessarily the Financial Times. It is relevant to understand what is happening in the real world with acquisitions, mergers, down-sizing, boardroom conflicts, etc. The more widely that you read the financial press, the more it will help you to understand and fully appreciate all of the many complex factors that affect companies and the selection and implementation of their strategies.

It is also recommended that you should keep yourself updated with latest information on exchange rates, interest rates, government policies, the state of the economy, and particularly what is happening in the business sectors concerning mergers and acquisitions. The acquisition of a competitor, or a hostile takeover bid is a very important strategic move. Acquisitions happen everyday in the real world and you can familiarise yourself with how these work by reading the business press.

Remember when you are reading this information that you will be playing a particular role in the exam. So you should be thinking to yourself 'how might they implement this' and 'what might a management accountants role be' rather than just thinking about whether it is a good strategy or not.

Obviously, news media is available in hard copy from shops but also most good newspapers have websites that give you the day's stories and also have searchable archives on past stories about the industry or specific firms within it.

Using the Internet

This is the most convenient and commonly used method of researching the industry, but as noted above, try to target the information you're looking for in order to avoid wasting time. Generally, you will be looking for the following sorts of information:

- Websites of firms similar to the one(s) in the pre-seen material. This can help you learn about the sorts of products and competitive strategies they follow and may also yield financial information that can be compared with the data in the pre-seen material.

- Trade journals of the industry in the pre-seen. This will provide information on real world environmental issues facing the business.

- Articles on the industry in journals and newspapers. These will keep you up to date on developments.

- Financial statements of real firms (often these can be downloaded from companies' websites free of charge).

You could review the accounts and establish:

- typical industry working capital ratios,
- margins,
- growth rates.

You may provide yourself with some 'normal' industry figures as a basis for any comparisons you may wish to make of the unseen material in due course. You should also review all the non-financial information provided, looking in particular for:

- new technological developments, new products
- the competitive situation

If companies can be identified that are in the same or similar industries to the industry in the case, then it is possible to gain much information from these websites.

It is not helpful, as some candidates and tutors have done, to concentrate on any one single company, however similar you believe that is to the case. The examination team have made it clear that cases are not likely to be based exclusively on just one real world company and hence data will differ from any sets of accounts that you may consider the case is based on.

Company websites of public companies in similar industries can provide the annual report and accounts, any press releases, publicity material and product descriptions, and detailed documentation on such matters as rights issues and share option schemes. Often they contain specially commissioned pieces of market research that you can download. However, it's worth remembering that this research is there to encourage investors to anticipate higher returns in the future and will tend to put an optimistic gloss on events. One very efficient way to use the internet for research is to set up Google alerts for the topics you're interested in. This will provide you with daily emails containing links to new information on your specified areas.

7 Ethical analysis

Ethical issues could relate to any of the following areas:

- corporate social responsibility;
- personal ethical behaviour of individuals in the case;
- business ethics.

Before the exam, you should take some time to remind yourself of CIMA's Guidelines on ethical conduct. You can download a copy of the Ethical Guidelines from CIMA's website, if you want to read the full text. Although these are useful, you must remember that the ethical issues in the exam are not necessarily ethical issues facing the management accountant, but more issues facing the business as a whole. An awareness of general 'corporate ethics' and 'corporate and social responsibility' will therefore be beneficial.

8 Position audit

Once you've analysed all of the above you're ready to carry out a position audit.

CIMA defines a position audit as:

Part of the planning process which examines the current state of the entity in respect of:

- resources of tangible and intangible assets and finance,
- products brands and markets,
- operating systems such as production and distribution,
- internal organisation,
- current results,
- returns to stockholders.

What you should be attempting to do is stand back so you can appreciate the bigger picture of the organisation. You can do this by considering four main headings – Strengths, Weaknesses, Opportunities and Threats. This is usually referred to as a SWOT analysis. Within your SWOT analysis you should look for:

- Threat homing in upon weakness – the potential for failure.
- Threat on a strength – should be able to defend against it but remember competencies slip.
- Opportunity on a strength – areas they should be able to exploit.
- Opportunity on a weakness – areas where they could exploit in the future if they can change.

In addition to preparing a SWOT analysis, it is useful to prepare a two-three page summary of your analysis. Try not to simply repeat information from the pre-seen but add value by including your thoughts on the analysis you've performed.

9 Main issues and précis

Once you've prepared your summary you are finally able to consider the key issues facing the organisation. Your conclusion on the main issues arising from the pre-seen will direct your focus and aid your understanding of issues in the exam.

Once you've got a list of the main issues, give yourself more time to think. Spend some time thinking about the case study, as much as you can. You don't have to be sitting at a desk or table to do this. You can think about the case study when you travel to work or in any spare time that you have for thinking.

- When new ideas come to you, jot them down.

- If you think of a new approach to financial analysis, carry out any calculations you think might be useful.

Remember, all of the above preparatory work enables you to feel as if you really are a management accountant working for this organisation. Without the prep, you're unlikely to be convincing in this role.

10 Summary

You should now understand what you need to do in order to familiarise yourself with the pre-seen sufficiently. Working through this chapter will produce quite detailed analysis. Chapter Six will attempt to summarise this into key conclusions.

Next steps:

(1) Ensure you have applied each stage of analysis to the MW pre-seen

(2) Produce a brief summary of the key issues facing MW. We will give you our opinion in the following chapter but you should write your own notes on this first.

Test your understanding answers

Exercise 1 – Basic Financial Analysis

Ratio	2014	2013
Revenue growth	4%	–
Operating profit margin	20.6%	20.6%
Receivables days	50	46
Payables days	40	38
Inventory days	30	29

Pilot exam – summary of the preseen

Chapter learning objectives

- To apply the techniques covered in the previous chapter to the pilot pre-seen.

1 Introduction

In the previous chapter we showed you some techniques to help you in your analysis of the pre-seen.

Once you have completed your analysis of the pre-seen for the pilot paper you can review this chapter to ensure you have identified the key points. We will take you through each exhibit highlighting the key conclusions before bringing this together into a summary using the SWOT framework.

2 Exhibit by exhibit analysis

The key issues and conclusions that could have been brought out of the pre-seen exhibits are as follows:

Reference material 1: Background

The Company

- MW is a small, family-run, animal feeds manufacturer based in the UK.

- Set up 6 years ago by Mr Harris, MW experienced particularly high growth up until 2012 but has experienced higher competition since then, which has limited growth.

- MW currently has two products – SHEEP and CHICKEN.

Marketing mix

- Product – MW's feeds are very high quality, especially with respect to nutritional value.

- Promotion – word of mouth (even by vets) and publicity via articles. MW also employs a part-time sales manager but it is unclear what they do.

- Price – we are not told the pricing strategy except that it is linked to the cost per unit. One would assume a standard mark up is used but we are not told this.

- Place – MW sells direct to farmers across the country and also to a major distributor.

Operations

- Recipes for the two products have not changed for 6 years.

- Key ingredients, R and S, are sourced from a single supplier, BF, who was recently taken over by a multinational.

- New R&D facility recently set up, increasing the likelihood of new products being announced in the unseen information for MW. If so, then this could have implications for production, marketing and finance.

Finance

- No debt finance. If MW wishes to grow in the future, then it may need to consider bank loans. We are told that Mr Harris has a good relationship with the bank manager.

- Significant dividend paid to Mr Harris, presumably the sole shareholder.

Management accounting

- No budgeting but do have standard cost cards.

Financial accounting

- Standard but basic accounting package used.

- Financial statements prepared externally.

- MW is a single entity so no group accounting aspects to worry about at present.

- No audit.

Reference material 2 – Article

MW products are praised for

- High nutritional and health value

- Can be blended effectively with other cheaper feeds

- Takes away the guess work for farmers trying to get an optimal blend of ingredients

Note: Given that the blends are based on standard ingredients is there a risk that rivals could develop a similar mix and erode MW's competitive advantage?

Reference material 3 – Standard cost cards

Costing system

- MW uses absorption costing

- Overheads are absorbed using direct labour hours

- Absorption rate calculated using budgeted sales volumes

- Inflation incorporated into estimated fixed overheads (the bulk of which is presumably rent and salaries)

Comments

- A rate per hour is suitable for absorbing some staff costs but a system based on floor area may be better for rent. Should they consider switching to an ABC system?

- Standard time to mix a bag of product has not been updated since 2012. Given the recipe hasn't changed, then this standard should still be valid.

- Similarly the variable OH rate per hour has not been updated since 2012. This is more likely to be out of date as (presumably) variable OH will have increased since then.

- No suggestion how they deal with over/under absorption of fixed overheads.

Reference material 4 – Newspaper article

The article starts by reinforcing some strengths of the firm, notably its close links with and responsiveness to local famers.

It then hints at a number of potential triggers for the unseen:

- The main thrust of the article is that Mark Harris plans to grow MW.

  This can often lead to working capital problems if growth is too rapid.

- The current product range is "limited", so could be told that MW is increasing the range.

  If so then there might be implications for marketing and organisational structure. If there are new products then they will need to be priced, presumably using the existing cost plus approach.

- MW plans to expand production facilities.

  This could raise issues such as financing, operations systems and quality.

- MW plans to recruit.

  This raises a range of HRM issues such as effective recruitment, induction, training and motivation.

- Depending on how large MW becomes there may be a need for additional specialist expertise at Board level as well as improvements to its management accounting systems – for example, the need for formal budgeting.

With each of the above potential triggers, you could recap underlying technical knowledge and consider how you could answer associated tasks – for example,

- which system of budgeting do you think would be most suitable for MW – incremental or ZBB or rolling or...?

- which organisational structure do you think would be most suitable for MW if they grow – functional or divisional or do you think the current entrepreneurial approach would still be effective?

Exploring potential triggers and tasks is continued in the next chapter.

Reference material 5 – Financial statements

Ratio analysis was performed in Chapter Five and the results are shown here:

Ratio	2014	2013
Revenue growth	4%	–
Operating profit margin	20.6%	20.6%
Receivables days	50	46
Payables days	40	38
Inventory days	30	29

Commentary:

- MW continues to be highly profitable and has paid a significant dividend.

- MW has strong overall cash flow and over £900,000 in the bank.

- Margins are stable, which is reassuring in a competitive market.

- Revenue growth was only 4% last year, indicating that competitive pressure is making growth difficult without either finding new products or new markets.

- Receivables and inventory days have increased, thus increasing the length of the cash operating cycle and increasing the risk that high growth could result in cash flow problems.

Reference material 6 – Industry Report

This exhibit gives useful information for identifying potential opportunities and threats.

Global trends

We are told that the industry is thriving, especially for niche products. However, there are many factors that indicate high levels of risk:

- Demand is driven mainly by economic growth but also regulations re animal husbandry (e.g. group housing for pigs) and the impact of disease (e.g. Schmallenberg virus affecting cattle, sheep and goats)

- Weather patterns can be a key issue for supply (e.g. grass production, growth of cereals and beans)

- Global supply and demand fluctuations can affect prices of feed ingredients (e.g. Chinese demand for soya)

UK statistics

We are given a number of useful statistics for estimating future growth:

- Overall output grew by 2.6% in 2014

- In 2014 all types of animal feed saw growth except for pig feed, which fell by 20%

- Highest growth in 2014 was in other feeds (24.7%), sheep feed (23.4%) and horse feed (18.1%). Poultry saw the lowest growth at 3.6%. Cattle feeds grew by 8.4%

- In 2015 growth of 1% expected for cattle and poultry feed and 0.5% for pig feed.

Given the above, it is recommended that MW look to extend their product range beyond just chicken and sheep to reduce the risk of their portfolio.

Other challenges

- Growth opportunities for feed that can prevent disease without the use of anti-biotics (EPRUMA)

- Sustainability becoming increasingly important (e.g. palm oil, soya). Areas of focus include use of certain agrochemicals, standards for responsible labour conditions, community relations, environmental responsibility as well as legal compliance and good business practice in the growing regions.

Expect to have to be able to discuss MW's commitment to sustainability.

3 SWOT analysis

A SWOT analysis is a useful tool to summarise the current position of the company. It is simply a listing of the following:

- The STRENGTHS of the organisation. These are internal factors that give the organisation a distinct advantage.

- The WEAKNESSES of the organisation. These are internal factors that affect performance adversely, and so might put the organisation at a disadvantage.

- The OPPORTUNITIES available. These are circumstances or developments in the environment that the organisation might be in a position to exploit to its advantage.

- The THREATS or potential threats. These are factors in the environment that present risks or potential risks to the organisation and its competitive position.

Strengths and weaknesses are internal to the organisation, whereas opportunities and threats are external factors.

A SWOT analysis can be presented simply as a list of strengths, followed by weaknesses, then opportunities and finally threats. It would be useful to indicate within each category which factors seem more significant than others, perhaps by listing them in descending order of priority. Alternatively a SWOT analysis, if it is not too long and excludes minor factors, can be presented in the form of a 2 × 2 table, as follows:

Strengths	Weaknesses
Opportunities	Threats

With this method of presentation, the positive factors (strengths and opportunities) are listed on the left and the negative factors (weaknesses and threats) are on the right.

Test Your Understanding

Prepare a SWOT analysis of MW based on the summary of each exhibit and the guidance above.

Strengths	Weaknesses
Opportunities	**Threats**

4 Summary

You should now be comfortable with all the key issues identified in the MW pre-seen and ready to start thinking about the exam.

Next steps:

(1) It is a good idea, once you have analysed the pre-seen, to brainstorm a list of possible triggers (what might happen) and tasks (what you have to do) which you may face in the exam.

This is NOT an exercise in question spotting as you cannot hope to simply guess the requirements and only study a limited amount of topics.

However this brainstorm will help you to think about how the pre-seen may relate to the competencies and may mean fewer complete surprises on the day of the exam.

Test your understanding answers

Test Your Understanding

Strengths	Weaknesses
• Strong reputation for quality of product, especially nutritional value • Strong customer focus – especially with local farmers • New R&D facility • Profitable • No gearing • Strong cash flow and cash rich	• Narrow product range • Lack of growth • Simplistic accounting systems • Over-reliance on sole supplier?
Opportunities	**Threats**
• Expand product range to other animals to reduce risk • Develop more products that help prevent disease • Expand production capacity • Increasing emphasis on sustainability	• Pressure to reduce prices by major distributor • Price increases from BF, given recent change in ownership • Rivals may successfully replicate MW's recipes, especially as they haven't changed in 6 years. • Price rises in raw ingredients due to fluctuations in global supply and demand

7

Practice triggers and tasks

Chapter learning objectives

- To understand how underlying knowledge from E1, P1 and F1 could be applied within the case study.

1 Introduction

In previous chapters you have been introduced to the concept of triggers and tasks and in Chapter Six we have helped you to prepare and analyse the pre-seen information for the pilot exam – MW. Before we think about the exam day itself we will do some practice exercises which will help you prepare for as many different scenarios as possible arising in the exam. This will also give you an opportunity to revise some key aspects of the syllabus and consider how they may be applied to the scenario. It is crucial that you go through this process to fully prepare yourself for the exam.

However, you need to be careful – this is NOT an exercise in question spotting. We are aiming to revise the knowledge required and practise the skills needed to perform well in any exam rather than guess what may come up. Any set of pre-seen exhibits can give rise to a huge range of possible tasks – we have only provided a sample here.

Once you understand the competencies by which this exam will be marked, are completely comfortable with the syllabus diagnostics at the beginning of Chapter Three and have thoroughly prepared the pre-seen information produced in Chapter Four then you are ready to continue with these exercises. Each task begins with a small scenario (or trigger) to introduce the topic and set the scene. You should be using the skills discussed in Chapter Eight to work through these tasks. These tasks are discrete – i.e. they do not follow on from each other but stand alone as sample exercises. Later on in this book we will consider how the tasks will flow into a complete exam.

Note: These task exercises are not related to each other. All you need to attempt this task is the pre-seen material and the additional material provided below. You should not make reference to any material provided for other practice tasks.

2 E1 – Organisational management

Exercise 1

The following email appeared in your inbox after lunch:

From: Mark Harris
Sent: Today, 3pm
Subject: Management meeting

The directors and managers spent all morning in a meeting. Normally these are short and productive but there was a lot of tension today. It seems the current plans to expand are causing some panic.

Mostly there is uncertainty over how much we're likely to sell and if production does greatly increase, or fluctuate, how we will keep an eye on inventory levels.

Can you email me and explain ways of predicting future demand? Also, who should be responsible for this?

I'd also like you discuss methods to manage inventory effectively and who should be tasked with this.

I'd like this as quickly as possible as I feel it's vital to keep the staff happy. We can't successfully expand without their support.

Many thanks,
Mark

Note: you could argue that forecasting demand covers both P1 and E1 syllabus areas. This illustrates how a single trigger and task could cover more than one underlying paper.

Exercise 2

Although you have only been with MW for a short time Mr Harris is impressed with your work. Never a man to hide his thoughts, he called you into his office last week to congratulate you on your 'fitting in with the company' and for your 'strong work ethic'.

He discussed the possibility of expanding the finance team with 3 new staff members and putting you in charge, and you agreed that you'd be happy for this to occur.

When you arrived at work this morning the following email was in your inbox:

From: Mark Harris
Sent: Yesterday, 10.06pm
Subject: Expansion of the finance function

Hello.

Planning to get together with the other managers this afternoon and discuss the potential expansion of the finance function. If they are agreeable I see no reason why we can't begin recruitment in the next few weeks.

Could you please supply me with an overview of the main activities carried out by a finance function in a company of our size? I just want a one sheet presentation outlining the key ideas that I can hand round to Mrs Harris and the other department managers. This can be in bullet format with a brief explanation underneath of how each point can be related to MW.

Once you get this to me, we can talk about sourcing the additional staff and how your new role will develop.

All the best,
Mark

---

3 P1 – Management accounting

Exercise 3

You arrive at work this morning and find the following graph on your desk:

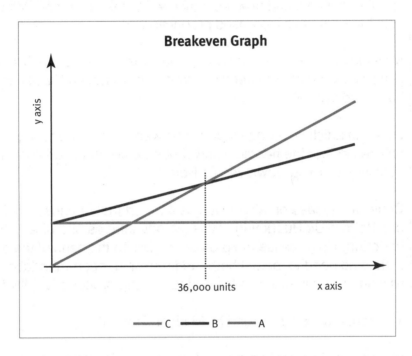

Attached to the graph is this note:

Hi.

I've left you a copy of a graph that Zoe gave me last night. It relates to her new plan to sell goat pellets. Apparently an accountant friend from university helped her prepare it. She said I can clearly see how profitable the project will be from this series of lines on a page. I really can't!

Zoe tells me this is a breakeven chart and mentioned something about a 25% margin of safety on the sales. Producing goat pellets will also increase our fixed costs as additional staff will need to be hired.

Could you give me an interpretation of this diagram so that I can discuss the project with her in greater detail? Please just send me an email explaining what breakeven is, why it's relevant to this new project and what the margin of safety means.

Thanks,
Mark

Exercise 4

You have received the following note from Mrs Harris, company director:

Mr Harris and I have just come back from a meeting with the bank manager. We were discussing our future plans to develop foodstuffs for other animals and how we may need to take on more staff to accommodate this increased production.

Mr Simmons, the bank manager, would like us to present him with a general budget of our spending plans and we haven't really decided how to do this yet.

I read an article in a trade journal last week about budgeting but can only remember the headline and vague details of the content. The headline was Top Down versus Bottom Up.

Could you please email me across a report that defines Top-Down and Bottom-Up Budgeting, gives the advantages and disadvantages of Bottom-Up (I realise the pros of one will be the cons of the other so there's no need to look at both) and makes a recommendation as to who should be involved in the budget-setting process for MW?

This report will only be read by Mark and me.

Please email it over to me by the end of the day if possible.

Regards,
Mary

4 F1 – Financial accounting

Exercise 5

When you arrived at work this morning the following email was in your inbox:

From: Mark Harris
Sent: Today, 9.45am
Subject: External audit

Good morning.

I was out at a dinner-dance with my wife last night and bumped into a man I went to school with. Haven't seen him in years! Apparently he runs a small business up north and even though he isn't legally obliged to do so, has his company externally audited every year. Says it's great for business but he was a bit vague with the detail.

I've always assumed having an external auditor would just be time consuming and costly.

Could you prepare me a quick report on what an external auditor's role actually is? Do they make sure our financial statements are 100% correct and ensure we're not open to fraud?

And what could be the benefits to MW of having our financial statements externally audited at this time of expansion?

Please drop me your response as quickly as possible. I'm heading off to a meeting later this afternoon and would like to take the report with me.

Many thanks,
Mark

Exercise 6

The following is an extract of an article that appeared in yesterday's local newspaper:

Biscuit Factory Reaches Breaking Point

Bonny Biscuits has come to the end of the road as they have been unable to appeal to the younger generation. The sugar-topped biscuit which was a staple for locals in the 60s and 70s has been losing market share over many years and the owners have finally decided to close the lid on their business.

Mr Black, the founder of the company stated he was sad to see the company go but would be glad to have a rest after all these years....

Mr Harris has sent you the following email:

From: Mark Harris
Sent: Today, 9.05am
Subject: Factory

Hello.

I have a quick query for you about assets.

I spoke to an estate agent friend last night who told me the Bonny Biscuit factory is up for sale. This could be great news as it would allow us to expand our business operations. He also reckons that, even though we wouldn't be buying it as an investment, it will be worth a lot more in a few years time because of the way the market is going.

If we have this factory on our books and the value shoots up in the future, can we revalue it and make our profits look good?

Could you please email me an overview of how this asset could be re-measured after initial inclusion in the accounts?

Many thanks,
Mark

---

5 Summary

You should better understand the wide range of possible tasks which you may encounter in the exam. You should also have a better appreciation of the level of detail required in your answers to score a high mark in the exam.

Next steps:

(1) Have you attempted all of the tasks in this chapter? Don't be tempted to look at the answers until you have, at the very least, made detailed notes on your response.

(2) If you struggled with any of these tasks, this may indicate a knowledge gap which you need to revisit.

Test your understanding answers

Exercise 1

Note: These suggested answers are indicative of what could be produced by a very competent student, in the time allowed, and would earn a good pass. They are not 'reference', or 'model', answers. Other, equally valid, points would receive credit. It is important that you attempt to produce your own answers and then reflect on whether you have addressed the requirement BEFORE reviewing these suggested solutions.

From: Accounts
Sent: Today, 4.30pm
Subject: Sales demand and inventory levels

Dear Mark,

Thank you for your email. Please find below a discussion of methods to forecast demand and manage inventory levels.

Forecasting demand

In this time of planned expansion it is vital that MW can forecast future demand, both for current products produced and for new products it is bringing to the market. A reliable estimate of sales will help with managing inventory and allow MW to decide whether it is worthwhile investing money in new products.

Miss Lyons, the sales manager, should be tasked with carrying out market research.

Forecasts can be based on historical data such as previous sales trends. Whilst this is useful for the chicken and sheep pellets, it will not give MW information on the new products it is developing. Miss Lyons should talk to current customers not only about our chicken and sheep pellets, but to see if they will be interested in MW's new animal feeds. Farm animal feed distributors could also be contacted to see if there is scope for new alliances to be formed.

Newspapers, trade journals and the internet can be reviewed on a regular basis to see if there are business opportunities that MW can take advantage of, or if current relationships may be at risk. Economic conditions will affect consumer confidence and buying behaviour.

A revenue analysis would be useful to see how much comes from MW's one major farm animal feed distributor. If MW is placing large reliance on their business and fluctuations in demand occur, MW's ability to trade could be adversely affected. The accounts department can do this alongside Miss Lyons.

Managing inventory

It is vital for MW to carefully manage inventory levels. Holding too much inventory or too little both carry significant risks.

With a large level of inventory, holding costs can be high and significant storage space may be required, which MW may not have access to. Also, since MW deals with perishable items, there is a risk of it having to be written off if not used in time.

On the other hand, too small an amount of inventory can delay production. If MW runs of out ingredients and does not fulfil a customer order in time it can lead to loss of goodwill. Since MW sells to a major farm animal food distributor it is vital that a good working relationship is maintained to ensure future orders and secure revenue.

There are 3 main types of inventory management that MW could consider.

- A **continuous** inventory system means that each new addition or withdrawal will be recorded as it occurs. A pre-determined quantity of inventory is ordered when inventory levels fall to a re-order level. A model called the Economic Order Quantity (EOQ) is used to determine the optimum re-order quantity and this model will minimise total inventory costs.

- A **periodic** inventory system does not keep inventory levels under constant review but it will be checked on a regular basis and a variable order placed depending on usage during the period.

- The **ABC** system is based on the theory that 80% of inventory usage can be accounted for by 20% of inventory items. The inventory is divided into different classifications (A, B and C) with category A being items of high value in terms of usage rate, and categories B and C for medium and lesser value items, where control is less vital.

Currently MW only has one large supplier, BF, for two key ingredients. With the plans to expand and produce different foods other suppliers may become important in time, but currently it is vital to manage this key supplier relationship.

Regular contact should be maintained with BF and regular reviews made of R and S inventories (a periodic inventory system). MW may want to consider having one point of contact to manage this supplier relationship. Perhaps Mr Webb, the production manager should handle this as he will already have an established working relationship with BF.

Please let me know if you require any further information.

Kind regards,
Accounts

Exercise 2

Main activities of a Finance Department

- Recording transactions on the accounting package software

  This is currently carried out by one accountant at MW but with the planned business growth a greater volume of transactions will occur and more staff may be needed.

- Supplying timely reports to management

  Reports supplied to management can help with strategy formulation and decision making. This can cover planning and control through to optimum use of resources and which product lines MW may wish to expand or reduce.

- Testing controls established by management

  Company directors are responsible for establishing a sound system of internal control to identify and mitigate risks. The finance department can assist in the implementation and testing of these controls to ensure they are functioning correctly e.g. controls to protect our customers' data.

- Carrying out investigations as required by management

  If special one off investigations arise such as investment appraisal for new factory premises, the finance function could prepare the analysis.

- Planning to ensure a company has appropriate and sufficient funding available

  MW has a high cash balance which can be utilised at this time of expansion but the finance function can also advise on other appropriate sources of funding, such as debt or equity. It is vital that there is enough cash available to cover expenditure, be it new premises, increased stock needs or research funding.

- Assisting in preparation of budgets

  Whilst MW currently has no formal annual budgeting process this may become necessary as product ranges are expanded. The accountants can help ensure budgets are prepared and circulated on a timely basis.

- Product costing and profit assessment

  Standard cost cards are currently produced for each product at the start of the financial year to aid determination of selling prices. The finance function can continue to prepare costing on this basis or provide a more detailed costing approach, allowing the examination of product profitability. The standard cost card currently uses some figures dating from 2012, so it would be appropriate to update these.

- Preparation of accounts

  Even though these are currently produced off-site by an external firm of accounts, an expansion of the in-house finance team could allow MW themselves to prepare their financial statements, potentially saving costs and keeping the function within our control.

- Inventory stock counts

  The finance function can also be present at stock counts, helping to assess the value of inventory. With perishable items being used and plans to produce a greater range of products, it is vital that these are valued appropriately in the accounts.

Exercise 3

To: Mark Harris
From: Accounts
Date: Today, 3pm
Subject: Breakeven and margin of safety

Dear Mark,

Thank you for your note. Please find below a brief explanation of breakeven and margin of safety and why it is important to consider for this new project.

Breakeven

Breakeven concerns the number of units of a product that must be sold to cover fixed and variable costs. In other words, a company must sell more than the break-even quantity to make a profit (in this case 720,000 bags of goat pellets).

First it is vital to work out the contribution of one unit of a product:

- Contribution = Selling price – Variable costs

MW already does this for sheep and chicken pellets, where variable costs include ingredients, labour and variable overheads. The same will apply to goat pellets.

The breakeven units can then be calculated by dividing the fixed costs by the contribution per unit of the goat pellets. As a simple example, if a product sells for £10 and the variable costs are £6, this leaves a contribution per unit of £4. If fixed costs increase by £4,000, then 1,000 units will have to be sold to cover the additional costs.

Interpretation of the graph

The x-axis represents the number of units sold and the y-axis is £.

- Line C represents the fixed costs associated with making goat pellets. Here that means additional salary.
- Line A is revenue, where the number of units has been multiplied by the selling price per unit.
- Line B represents the total cost of production (fixed + variable).

Where lines A and B intersect is the breakeven point.

Sales of 36,000 units will therefore recover all costs of production, including the additional salary costs. Any sales above this number of units will result in profit.

Our 2014 figures show expected production of 60,000 bags for chicken pellets and 75,000 bags for sheep pellets, so it must be considered whether or not the sale of 36,000 bags of goat pellets is reasonable. It would take 6 months at current sales figures to sell this many sheep pellets, for example.

The fixed cost of the machine, selling price and variable costs used for the graph must be obtained to allow assessment of their reasonableness. Knowing the selling price used will also allow consideration of whether the market will pay this price and hence, whether 36,000 bags can be sold.

Margin of safety

A margin of safety is the difference between the budgeted level of sales and the breakeven point.

Since MW currently has no formalised budgeting process it is important to consider the realism of projected figures. The larger the margin of safety, the more likely it is that a profit will be made. Margin of safety is often expressed as a percentage of projected sales.

- Margin of safety = (Budgeted sales – Breakeven sales)/Budgeted sales

In the case of the goat pellets, the 25% margin of safety figure means budgeted sales can fall by a quarter before it no longer makes a profit. To get a 25% margin Zoe has budgeted sales of 48,000 bags.

I hope this explanation is helpful. Should you wish for further clarification please let me know.

Kind regards,

Accounts department

Exercise 4

To: Mary Harris
From: Accounting Department
Date: Today, 4.03pm
Subject: Budgetary participation

Dear Mrs Harris,

Please find below a report that summarises the relative advantages and disadvantages of bottom-up budgeting, and makes a recommendation as to who should be involved in the budget-setting process at MW.

If you have any queries regarding the following, please do not hesitate to get in touch.

Kind regards,
Accounting Department

REPORT

Introduction – Budget participation

Top-Down Budgeting is where a budget is set by top level management without allowing the final budget holder to participate in the process. Bottom-Up Budgeting is where budget holders are given the opportunity to participate in setting their own budgets.

Bottom-up budgeting

Advantages

- Bottom-up budgeting can increase staff motivation. Their participation in setting the budget makes them feel more 'ownership' of the final budget, which can lead to working harder to achieve company goals.

- This style of budgeting also provides better information as staff in each department will be more familiar with their own line of work.

- Staff should gain a greater understanding of the budgeting process and this understanding can strengthen their commitment to projects.

- Communication between departments is enhanced, building stronger working relationships.

- Senior management may have more time to concentrate on higher level company strategy, as the details of the budget are taken care of at a lower level.

Disadvantages

- Whilst bottom-up budgeting can give senior management more time to concentrate on higher level strategy, it risks them losing touch with the day-to-day running of the business and fearing a loss of control.

- Managers may be tempted to concentrate on the needs of their own department rather than the business as a whole, resulting in dysfunctional decision making.

- If staff do not have the skill or experience to set budgets, they may make ill-informed decisions.

- Bottom-up budgeting can be a time consuming process, removing focus from the smooth running of the business.

- When managers have the chance to set their own targets they may introduce 'budgetary slack', choosing targets that are easy to achieve in order to 'look good' or earn bonuses.

Recommended budgetary process for MW

Since MW have not previously been involved in a detailed budgeting process, it is recommended that bottom-up budgeting is introduced for now.

While there are only 2 managers in the business it might be a good opportunity to take advantage of their detailed knowledge of the running of MW. Such a small group will also be able to communicate effectively and the close working relationships already established should lead to cooperation in the budgeting process.

It is recommended that both directors are involved in the initial budgeting process to guide the overall company strategy. Mr Webb should represent production and distribution as he will have intimate knowledge of both departments and the needs of his 22 staff. Miss Lyons, the sales manager, should be present as she will have projections for the future growth of the business. Zoe should also be present to discuss research and development funding needs, and the finance function should be represented to offer guidance during the budget setting process.

Exercise 5

Role of the external auditor

An external auditor is not employed to ensure financial statements are 100% correct or to prevent fraud:

- Their role is to form an opinion on whether financial statements are prepared in all material respects, in accordance with the applicable financial reporting framework.

- They will obtain reasonable assurance on whether financial statements are free from material misstatement – whether due to fraud or error.

- So whilst it is not their role to prevent fraud, their work could uncover it. Often, knowing financial statements are subject to the scrutiny of external auditors can act as a deterrent to those who would commit fraud.

In particular an auditor will evaluate whether:

- financial statements adequately disclose the significant accounting policies

- accounting policies selected are consistently applied and appropriate

- accounting estimates are reasonable

- information is relevant, reliable, comparable and understandable

- financial statements provide adequate disclosures to enable users to understand the effects of material transactions and events; and

- appropriate terminology is used.

Benefits to MW of having an external audit

An external auditor offers an independent opinion on the financial statements which can give comfort to the users of those financial statements and assist them in their decision making.

Key users of the Financial Statements are as follows:

- The bank:

  At this time of expansion, MW may need loans from the bank. Whilst MW has a good working relationship with the bank manager, it will offer the bank additional assurance that their debt is secure and that MW can repay charges as they fall due.

- New staff:

  In expanding the business and advertising for staff, people applying to work in the company will want to be assured of job security and that the company will continue as a going concern.

- Potential investors:

  If it was felt that equity finance may be sought in the future, whether from family or external investors, an audited set of accounts will help them reach an investment decision.

Other factors to consider

As MW currently sends its accounting information to an external firm, an audit will help MW directors feel secure that the financial statements are prepared in accordance with accounting standards and that accounting policies and estimates are used appropriately.

The external auditor can provide assurance on our current depreciation policy and the policy that may be adopted for new assets acquired.

There are complex accounting treatments concerning research and development costs in terms of which need to be capitalised and which expensed. An external auditor would be able to advise on appropriate treatment.

Food stuffs are perishable items and auditors can provide comfort over the valuation of inventory, especially in light of the expansion plans and new lines of inventory.

Conclusion

In conclusion, there are many benefits to be gained from the use of external auditors and the cost may not be prohibitive. Please let me know if you require further research on a suitable audit firm.

Exercise 6

To: Mark Harris
From: Accounts
Date: Today, 2pm
Subject: IAS 16

Dear Mark,

Thank you for your mail.

The issues you are referring to are dealt with by IAS 16 which looks at subsequent measurement of tangible non-current assets. IAS 16 requires that entities adopt either the cost model or the revaluation model.

Cost model

This is where an asset is recorded at cost and the book value will be cost less accumulated depreciation, less accumulated impairment losses.

Revaluation model

In this case, the book value is the fair value (that is 'the price that would be received to sell an asset or paid to transfer a liability in an orderly transaction between market participants at the measurement date') less accumulated depreciation, less accumulated impairment losses.

Revaluation must be carried out by a professionally qualified valuer, with 'sufficient regularity', and applied to all items in the same class. 'Sufficient regularity' is determined by the volatility of the fair values – the more volatile, the more frequent the revaluations.

Effect on profit

A revaluation will not improve the profit figure in the Statement of Profit or Loss.

If the new factory increases in value and the revaluation model is chosen, the following steps must occur:

- The asset cost is to be restated to the revalued amount, increasing the figure for tangible non-current assets.
- The entry for accumulated depreciation is reversed.

- The increase in the cost account and the existing depreciation are moved to the revaluation reserve. The revaluation reserve appears in the equity section of the statement of financial position.

- The new asset value will then be depreciated over the remaining useful economic life. If the remaining life is unchanged but the book value is greater than before, the depreciation figure taken to the profit and loss account will be greater than before.

- With a depreciating asset, a company is allowed to gradually release the revaluation reserve into retained earnings over the life of the asset. This is done by comparing the difference in the depreciation charge on the original asset value and the depreciation charge on the revalued amount.

I hope the above is of some help to you in explaining what would happen in the future if the factory increases in value and the revaluation method is chosen. Please let me know if you require any further explanation.

Kind regards,
Accounts department

8

Exam day techniques

Chapter learning objectives

- To develop a carefully planned and thought through strategy to cope with the three hours of exam time.

1 Exam day strategy

Once you have studied the pre-seen, learnt the three subject syllabi thoroughly and practised lots of exercises and mocks, you should be well prepared for the exam.

However, it is still important to have a carefully planned and thought through strategy to cope with those three hours of exam time.

This chapter takes you through some of the key skills to master to ensure all your careful preparation does not go to waste.

2 Importance of time management

Someone once referred to case study exams as "the race against time" and it's difficult to imagine a more accurate description. Being able to do what the examiner is wanting is only half of the battle; being able to deliver it in the time available is another matter altogether. This is even more important than in previous exams you may have faced because each section in the real exam is now timed and that once that time is up you will be moved on. Case study is not like a traditional exam where you can go back to a question if you get extra inspiration or feel you have some time left over. You have to complete each task within the time stated.

For this reason, time management is a key skill required to pass the Case Study Examination.

Successful time management requires two things:

- A tailored time plan – one that plays to your personal strengths and weaknesses; and
- Discipline in order to stick to it!

Time robbers

There are a number of ways in which time can be wasted or not used effectively in the Case Study Examination. An awareness of these will help to ensure you don't waste time in your exam.

Inactive reading

The first part of each task must be spent actively reading, processing the information and considering the impact on the organisation, how the issues link together and what could be done to resolve them. You may not have time to have a second detailed read and so these thoughts must be captured first time around.

Too much time spent on presentation

You will be writing your answer in software with some similarities to Microsoft Word however the only functions available are

- Cut
- Copy
- Paste
- Undo
- Redo
- Bold
- Italic
- Underline

The temptation to make various words bold or italics or underlined, is very hard to resist. But, resist you must! There are very few marks available for having a response that is well presented, and these finer details will be worth nothing at all.

Being a perfectionist

Students can often spend such a long time pondering about what to write that over the course of a 3 hour exam, over half of it is spent staring into space.

As you are sitting a computer exam you not only spend time pondering, but also have the ability to delete so can change your mind several times before settling on the right word combinations. Just focus on getting your points down and don't worry about whether they could have been phrased better.

Although do bear in mind that the marker has to be able to read and understand your answer, so do write in clear English.

Too much detail on earlier parts of the requirement

As we've said earlier, not finishing answers is a key reason for failing the Case Study Examination. One of the main reasons why students fail to finish a section is a lack of discipline when writing about an issue. They feel they have to get all of their points down rather than selecting the better points and moving on. If a task requires you to discuss three different areas it is vital that you cover all parts adequately.

Too much correction

Often students can reread paragraphs three or more times before they move on to writing the next part of their answer. Instead, try to leave the read through until the final few minutes of the task and try to correct as many obvious errors as possible. The CIMA marker will be reading and marking your script on screen and it is harder to read and understand the points you are making if there are many typing errors.

3 Assimilation of information

One of the most challenging things to deal with in a case study examination is the volume of information which you have available. This is particularly difficult when you have both pre-seen and unseen information to manage and draw from. It is important that you refer to relevant pre-seen information in your responses as well as incorporating the unseen information.

The key things that you need to do to assimilate the information effectively and efficiently are:

- Read about and identify each event

- Consider what the issue is

- Evaluate the impact of the issue. Who is affected, by how much are they affected and what would happen if no action was taken?

- Determine the most useful and relevant exhibits from the pre-seen

Capturing all of your thoughts and ideas at this stage can be difficult and time consuming.

The following section on planning your answer will show you how to do this effectively without wasting time or effort.

4 Planning your answers

In section 2 of this chapter we saw how important it was to manage your time in the exam to ensure you're able to complete all of the necessary stages in the preparation of your answer.

One important aspect of your exam is planning your answer. Sitting the Case Study Exam is not as straight forward as turning up, reading the requirements, and then writing your answer.

If you do attempt to write without any form of content plan, your response will lack direction and a logical flow, it won't fully address the key points required and any recommendations will lack solid justification. It is for this reason that time should be specifically allocated to planning the content of your answers.

Given the preparation you've done before the exam, reading the unseen can often feel like a firework display is happening in your brain; each new piece of information you read about triggers a series of thoughts and ideas.

The planning process must therefore begin as soon as you start reading the unseen information. Every second counts within the case study exam and so it's important to use all of your time effectively by capturing the thoughts as they come to you.

To make sure the time spent now is of use to you throughout the task, you will need consider carefully how best to document your thoughts. You will be provided with an on-screen notes page ('scratchpad') as well as a wipe-clean laminated notes page and marker pen. Any method you adopt to plan must be concise whilst still allowing you to capture all of your ideas and see the bigger picture in terms of how the issues interrelate with one another (see additional guidance below). Furthermore, the method must suit you! Everyone is different and what might work for one person could be a disaster for another. For example, some people prefer to work with lists, others with mind maps.

Most people find that some form of central planning sheet (to enable the bigger picture to be seen) is best. How you prepare the central planning sheet is a matter of personal preference and we've given illustrations of two different methods below. Practise each one to find out which you prefer and then tailor it further to settle on something that works for you.

Method 1 – The ordered list

This process is ideally suited to people who prefer lists and structure.

Step 1:

- Begin by reading everything in the task exhibit
- Ensure you have identified all aspects of the task and then write this on the left hand side of your planning sheet

Step 2:

- Read everything in the trigger exhibit, making notes next to the relevant task

Step 3:

- Review your list to identify any linkages to information provided in the pre-seen and note next to the task on your planning sheet

Step 4:

- Brainstorm any technical knowledge you can use in responding to the task and note this on your planning sheet

Illustration 1 – Planning

On Monday morning your boss arrived in work full of enthusiasm for a new business venture he had thought of over the weekend. This was in response to a conversation that had taken place at Friday night drinks when the CEO expressed concern that she felt the business was stagnating and needed some new products to rekindle customer interest.

Your boss needed to harness his ideas and put together an outline plan for a mid-morning coffee meeting with the CEO. Typically, the idea had germinated without sufficient thought and you were asked to consider the critical factors that needed to be considered in launching the new product and write a briefing document for the meeting.

Requirement:

Prepare a plan for your briefing document.

Solution

Critical factors	Goals and objectives	Skills and experience	Finance	Marketing and sales
New product	Matches mission and objectives?	Experience in manufacturing?	Available finance?	Advertising
	Strengths?	Available labour?	Investment?	Social media
			Working capital?	Website?
Technical content?				4Ps

Method 2 – The extended mind map

This process is ideally suited to those who prefer pictures and diagrams to trigger their thoughts.

Step 1:

- Read the unseen information and identify the key tasks required
- As you read, write each task in a "bubble" on your planning sheet.

Step 2:

- Keep adding each new part of the task you identify to your sheet. At the end you should have a page with a number of bubbles dotted about.

Step 3:

- Review your bubbles to identify any linkages to the trigger information or pre-seen exhibits. Add any relevant information to your planning sheet in a bubble attached to the appropriate part of the task.

Step 4:

- Review the task bubbles and brainstorm any relevant knowledge which you can use in responding to the task. Add this to bubbles attached to the task.

With detailed information provided in the exam it would be very likely that your brain would think of a wide range of ideas which, if left uncaptured, would be forgotten as quickly as you thought of them.

This is where mind mapping comes in handy. You would not of course need to draw one as neat as this and feel free to add colours or graphics to help your thought processes.

Have a go!

Why not try putting your thoughts on the previous illustration into a mind map like the one above?

Some additional guidance

(1) This is perhaps the hardest part of the exam; as soon as you tell your brain it needs to come up with some ideas, it very often refuses to cooperate! Practice makes perfect so working through the exercises in Chapter 7 and attempting mock exams will really help your brain to deliver ideas when you need it to.

(2) Don't simply view technical models as something that must be included to tick a box if explicitly requested in the requirements. Instead use the models to help analyse the issues, suggest solutions or generate ideas. They were developed to be useful!

(3) If you start looking at one of the task requirements and are stuck for ideas, don't waste time staring into space. Move on to the next part of the task (but not onto the next task itself as you won't be able to return) and you'll find the creative juices soon start flowing.

5 Communication skills

The Case Study examinations aim to test a wide range of skills and you may be required to communicate in many different ways to various different audiences, each with different information needs. How well you communicate will be marked as **both** part of the integration marks but also as part of the people skills, because communication skills is a subset of people skills. Some of the formats you may need to use are shown below.

Slide presentation

If a slide presentation is called for, your answer need only consist of the bullet points that would appear on each slide. Read the requirement carefully as guidance will be given on how many slides to prepare and the maximum number of bullets on each slide. Most likely this would be 2 slides, with a maximum of 5 bullets on each slide (or you may just be asked for 10 bullet points in total). You will not need to prepare speaker notes. You do not need to layout your answer as a slide (i.e. you don't need to draw a box). Simply noting the bullets will be sufficient.

Illustration 2 – Slides

A typical layout for the presentation of slides should be:

Slide 1

Title

- XX
- XX
- XX
- XX
- XX

Slide 2

Title

- XX
- XX
- XX
- XX
- XX

An email

A requirement to draft an email may be in response to a specific question raised by an individual within the unseen information, or perhaps even in response to an email that is presented within the unseen.

If an email response is required the email header will already be set up for you in the answer box.

If you are asked to write an email, then you should write short sentences (the number of which may well be specified in the requirement) and NOT brief bullet points. The headings shown in the above illustration (who the email is to, from etc) may well be given as a proforma in the exam.

A letter

Exactly the same as for an email but laid out in letter format. That means you should include a space for an address, a date, state to whom the letter is addressed and a summary of what the letter is regarding.

The letter should be signed off in the normal business fashion, unless you are told otherwise.

Illustration 3 – Letter

A typical layout for the presentation of a letter should be:

> **Address**
>
> **Date**
>
> **Dear X**
>
> **Title**
>
> Content of your answer to the requirement using short sentences or bullet points as instructed.
>
> Yours sincerely,
>
> A Management Accountant

A report

In the pilot exam a commonly requested format is a report. This is likely to be an internal report but should still follow an appropriate and formal structure. The exact headings in your report will needed to be tailored to the exact task requirements but the following example is a good start:

You might also be asked for sections of a report and not the whole thing.

Illustration 4 – Report

A typical layout for a report should be:

> **Title: A report on the implementation of Total Quality Management**
>
> Introduction
>
> Brief background/context for requirement
>
> Main report content broken down using further sub-headings
>
> Conclusion
>
> Key conclusions and recommendations

6 Writing style

Introduction

Writing style is something that develops over time. It is influenced by your education and experiences. To some it comes easily, they enjoy words – but remember, you are not looking to win any prizes in literature. It's about putting facts, ideas and opinions in a clear, concise, logical fashion. Some students get very worried about their writing styles. As a general rule you should try to write as you would talk.

Logical flow

A typical point starts with a statement of fact, either given in the case or derived from analysis – 'what?'

This can then be followed by an interpretation – 'so what?'

This can then lead to an implication – 'now what?', or 'what next?'

For example:

(1) What? – The net relevant cash flow for the project is positive.

(2) So what? – Suggesting we should go ahead with the project.

(3) Now what? – Arrange board meeting to discuss strategic implications.

A similar structure can be obtained using the Socratic approach – what, why, how?

- So what?

- Why should we use it?

- How does it work?

Who is reading the response?

Failure to pitch the level correctly will inevitably result in failure to communicate your ideas effectively, since the reader will either be swamped with complexity, or bored with blandness. The recipients of the report should also dictate the level of tact required.

Tactless	Tactful
The directors have clearly made errors	There were other options open to the board that, with hindsight, would have been beneficial
The marketing director is responsible for this disastrous change in strategy	The board should consider where this went wrong? It would appear that the marketing department may have made some mistakes

Making your response easy to read

To ensure that the marker finds your answers accessible and easy to read, you should try to do the following:

- Use short words, short sentences, short phrases and short paragraphs. If you are adopting the 'what, so what, what now' approach, then you could have a paragraph containing three sentences. The next point can then be a new paragraph, also containing three sentences.

- Use the correct words to explain what you mean! For example, students often get confused between:

  - recommendations (what they should do – actions) and options (what they could do – possibilities).

  - objectives (what we want to achieve – the destination) and strategies (how we intend to achieve them – the route).

- Avoid using vague generalisations. Too often students will comment that an issue will "impact" on profit rather than being specific about whether profit will increase or decrease (or even better still, trying to quantify by how much). Other common phrases which are too vague include "communicate with" (you need to say specifically what should be discussed) and "look in to" (how should an option be looked in to?)

- Avoid unnecessary repetition. This can either be of information from the exam paper (pre-seen or unseen), of discussion within the report (in particular between what is said in one section and another) or can relate to the words that you use. Some students fall into the trap of thinking that writing a professional report means simply writing more words to say the same thing! The issue is quality not quantity.

  For example, compare the following:

  - 'I, myself, personally'   OR 'I'
  - 'export overseas'   OR 'export'
  - 'green in colour'   OR 'green'

- Watch your spelling – this may seem a small and unimportant point, but poor spelling makes a document seem sloppy and may convey an impression that the content is as loose as the general appearance! Poor spelling interrupts the marker as they read your report, so there is the danger that they conclude that it did not have a logical flow.

- Recommendations – be decisive – do not 'sit on the fence' or ask for more information. Make a clear recommendation based on the information you have and justify why you have chosen that course of action.

Exercise 1

This exercise will get you thinking about what makes a well written script. The technical content of the requirement is not relevant – we are focusing on writing style and flow.

> The risk committee of X plc met to discuss a report by its risk manager. The report focused on a number of risks that applied to a chemicals factory recently acquired in another country.
>
> She explained that the new risks related to the security of the new factory in respect of burglary, the supply of one of the key raw materials that experienced fluctuations in world supply and also an environmental risk.
>
> The environmental risk was with respect to the possibility of poisonous emissions from the new factory. The CEO who chaired the risk committee, said that the factory was important to him for two reasons. First, he said it was strategically important to the company. Second, it was important because his own bonuses depended upon it. He said that he knew from the report what the risks were, but that he wanted somebody to explain to him what strategies they could use to manage the risks. 'I don't get any bonus at all until we reach a high level of output from the factory,' he said. 'So I don't care what the risks are, we will have to manage them.'

You have been asked to outline strategies that can be used to manage risk and identify, with reasons, an appropriate strategy for each of the three risks facing the new venture.

Requirement:

Consider these two responses and note the positive and negative aspects of each.

Answer 1

Introduction

Risk can be managed using the following strategies.

- **Transfer** the risk to another organisation for example by buying insurance. This is usually cost effective where the probability of the risk is low but the impact is potentially high.
- **Avoid** the risk altogether by withdrawing completely from the risky activity. This is done where the risk is high probability and high frequency and so it is too costly to reduce the risk sufficiently.
- **Reduce** the risk by implementing controls or by diversification.
- **Accept** the risk without taking any further steps to mitigate it. For this to be acceptable the frequency and the impact of the risk must place the risk within the risk appetite of the company.

Risk of burglary

It is usual to insure against burglary an example of the transfer strategy. This is because of the high impact of burglary.

It is also usual to put safeguards in place such as security guards because of the probability of burglary. This is an example of risk reduction.

Raw materials supply fluctuation

Depending on the cost benefit analysis the company could chose to transfer the risk by entering into forward contracts to purchase the materials.

There will be a cost associated with this and it will lower but not remove the risk associated with supply and price fluctuations. They may choose to accept the risk as part of the operational risk associated with their industry.

Environmental risk

The company should take reasonable steps to reduce the chance poisonous emissions. It should use appropriate technology and controls to reduce the risk.

Risks cannot be completely eliminated so if the poisonous emissions could give rise to significant costs it should also purchase insurance and transfer the risk.

Answer 2

Risk is managed by this:

(1) Identify the risk. This is by brainstorming all the things that the risk can be.

(2) Risk assessment. We won't know this properly until afterwards.

(3) Risk Profiling. This is decided on consequences and impact.

(4) Risk quantification. This can be average loss or it can be largest loss.

(5) Risk consolidation which will depend on the risk appetite and diversification.

The risks at the factory are:

- The main risk at the factory is environmental risk. You can't do anything about this risk because global warming is because of everyone.

- The big risk is that the CEO is "I don't care what the risks are" this will need to have the risk awareness embedded in and the tone at the top.

- The other risk is that the CEO could manipulate the output levels to get his bonus. This needs to be looked at seriously because he is also on the risk committee and the remuneration committee and he is not independent and that should be a NED.

7 Summary

You should have an appreciation of some of the issues you may encounter in the exam and some possible techniques to overcome these.

Next steps:

(1) In the next two chapters we will present the unseen and guide you through the process of producing an answer. It is worth ensuring you can log on to the Pearson Vue site now and make sure you have registered for the practice case study exam. It is advisable to familiarise yourself with the software as much as possible.

(2) As you are about to embark on a full attempt at the pilot paper it is a good time to revisit previous chapters and ensure you are comfortable with all of the material so far before proceeding.

Test your understanding answers

The first solution has several positive aspects:

- Brief introduction linking to requirement
- Overview of model with explanation and clear examples
- Specific points from scenario addressed
- Headings clearly signpost the answer
- Appropriate language

There are some areas which could be improved:

- Specific reference to the company name
- More explicit use of the information from the scenario

The second solution is not as strong as the first. Some of the main criticisms:

- Main options available are not clearly explained
- No attempt to introduce the answer
- Inappropriate language for a formal report/response
- Lack of tact regarding the CEO – the intended audience!!

As a piece of writing there is not much to say from a positive perspective except:

- Clear structure
- Writing is concise (but probably a bit too brief)

Pilot exam – unseen information

Chapter learning objectives

1 Introduction

In the Operational level case study practice exam the first screen you are presented with shows the number of tasks and the designated time allocations:

This examination is structured as follows:

Section	Number of tasks	Timing of section
1	1	45 minutes
2	1	45 minutes
3	1	45 minutes
4	1	45 minutes

The time available in each section is for reading, planning and writing your response(s).

This information will be available for you to access during the examination by clicking on the pre-seen button.

2 Unseen information – triggers and tasks

The pilot case study then continues and you are presented with the following triggers and tasks.

Note that in the exam these are not labelled as "tasks" or "triggers" but are presented simply as exhibits, emails, articles and so on. Similarly exhibits are not numbered. We have added these labels to make navigation and understanding easier.

Exhibit 1 – Trigger

Today is the 24th May 2015.

You have just received the following extract from the board meeting minutes from 15th May 2015:

MW
Meeting minutes
15th May 2015
Next meeting: 15th June 2015

Research and development:

Mr Harris was pleased to report to the meeting that two new animal feed products have now been developed by the research and development facility – to be known as HORSE and GOAT. There is currently spare capacity within the factory and therefore certainly initially these new products can be produced without compromising existing production and with little impact on fixed costs. At the moment Mr Harris is in negotiation with a potential customer for HORSE and GOAT. No contract has been signed yet – although it is anticipated that sales will start at a relatively low level and build gradually.

Costing information:

Mr Harris reported that MW currently uses a simplified absorption costing approach to calculate an estimated standard cost for a single bag of product, whereby total fixed overheads are estimated at the start of the year and an absorption rate per direct labour hour is calculated. Mr Harris reported that he has heard that activity based costing (ABC) is an alternative method to use in calculating standard cost for bag of product. Together with the accountant he will explore this further.

Subsequent to the Board meeting held on 15 May 2015, Mr Harris informed you about wanting to explore the possibility of using ABC. You have already undertaken some work on this and have completed a schedule showing the calculation of standard costs per bag for each product under the two different costing approaches. This has been based on your best estimate of the data needed as you have not had a great deal of time. You sent the schedule to Mr Harris without any form of explanation.

The schedule can be found by clicking on the reference materials button above.

Note: this schedule is shown in the next exhibit.

Exhibit 2 – Costing schedules

Base data:

	CHICKEN	SHEEP	HORSE	GOAT
Number of bags of estimated production on an annual basis	60,000	75,000	5,000	12,000

Total estimated fixed production overhead is £930,00.

Total direct labour hours are now 29,350.

Absorption rate is now £31.69 per direct labour hour.

Table 1: – on MW's traditional method – absorption of fixed production overhead on a direct labour hour basis:

	CHICKEN £	SHEEP £	HORSE £	GOAT £
Direct ingredients cost (Note 1)	6.10	9.80	21.00	15.00
Direct labour cost	1.50	2.00	3.50	3.00
Variable overhead cost	0.90	1.20	2.10	1.80
Total variable production cost	**8.50**	**13.00**	**26.60**	**19.80**
Fixed overhead (on a direct labour hour basis)	4.75	6.34	11.09	9.51
Total estimated production cost for a bag	**13.25**	**19.34**	**37.69**	**29.31**

Note 1:

The direct ingredients cost is based upon the following quantities of ingredients

	CHICKEN kg	SHEEP kg	HORSE kg	GOAT kg
Quantity of ingredients	20	38	75	48

Table 2: – activity based costing method – absorption of fixed production overheads on a cost driver basis:

	CHICKEN £	SHEEP £	HORSE £	GOAT £
Total variable production cost	8.50	13.00	26.60	19.80
Fixed overhead:				
Set up costs	1.56	1.29	8.00	4.17
Ingredients handling costs	2.22	2.80	7.40	4.93
Inspections	0.22	0.19	0.20	0.08
Other overhead (on a direct labour hour basis)	0.80	1.42	3.23	2.62
Total estimated production cost for a bag	**13.30**	**18.70**	**45.43**	**31.60**

Exhibit 3 – Task

Upon receipt of your costing schedule Mr Harris sends you the following email:

> **From:** Mark Harris, mh@mw.co.uk
> **Sent:** 24th May 2015, 10:01 a.m.
> **Subject:** Costing
>
> Thank you for the costing schedule that you sent me. I have to admit I know very little about ABC and the basis of your calculations, although I am surprised to see how different the costs of a bag are:
>
> It would be very useful for me and also for Mr Webb, the Production Manager, if you could prepare us a report which covers the following:
>
> - some detail regarding how an activity based costing system differs from a traditional absorption costing system
> - the advantages and disadvantages to our business of using ABC
> - the implication of using ABC on our costing information; and
> - the likely difficulties we might encounter switching to activity based costing.
>
> Many thanks
> **Mark Harris**
> Director
> MW
> E: mh@mw.co.uk
> T: 0151 266 3114

Exhibit 4 – Combined trigger and task

One month later on 24th June 2015 the products HORSE and GOAT are now in production.

Mr Harris sends you the following email:

From: Mark Harris, mh@mw.co.uk
Sent: 24th June 2015, 10:15 a.m.
Subject: Property and recruitment

As you know we signed the contract with the local customer last month and HORSE and GOAT are now in the market place. However, word seems to have got out about the nutritional quality of the new products and I have been approached by a major national animal feed distributor to sell these products to them. As it stands we would currently not be able to fulfil any significant additional orders based on existing capacity, which means that we need to expand.

There is a factory for sale next door which could be used to increase our production capacity and I am currently looking into acquiring it. Clearly any expansion would mean that we will need a recruitment campaign to employ new staff with the correct skills, which is something that I have never had to do on this scale before. I have heard that online recruitment is very effective when recruiting on a large scale, but please could you advise me if this is the case and also whether there are any other recruitment options that might be suitable. It's important that we employ the right people first time.

The factory will cost £1,500,000 (which is £500,000 for the land and £1,000,000 for the factory building). Professional fees of £150,000 will need to be paid on this purchase. A significant investment in plant and equipment is also going to be needed of approximately £1,500,000. We currently rent our existing factory and warehouse and so this is the first time that the business has owned such significant assets. I'm interested to know how in particular the new property asset will affect our financial statements and it's effect on the profit of MW in the future.

Mark Harris
Director
MW
E: mh@mw.co.uk
T: 0151 266 3114

Exhibit 5 – Combined trigger and task

A week later on 1st July 2015 Mr Harris sends you the following email:

From: Mark Harris, mh@mw.co.uk
Sent: 1st July 2015 10:15 a.m.
Subject: Budgets

Thank you for the report that you sent me regarding recruitment for our new production facility and the information on the impact of the new assets on the financial statements.

Whilst I was reading it through it struck me that given the growth that the business is going through we ought to be thinking about using a more formal budgetary control system then we currently have. Up until now I've been happy that as long as I had an idea of the cost of producing a bag of CHICKEN and a bag of SHEEP to allow me to set a price and we have money in the bank that we weren't going far wrong.

However, I really don't think the business can continue this way and therefore I am keen to understand more about the benefits to us of setting more formal budgets and the different approaches to budget setting that might be appropriate for MW.

I'd also like you to explain the types of individual budget that might be appropriate to us, giving examples of the information required to create them.

No need for a report, please could you just respond by email.

Many thanks
Mark Harris
Director
MW
E: mh@mw.co.uk
T: 0151 266 3114

Exhibit 6 – Trigger

Four weeks later, after your annual leave, you return to work to find the following email from Mr Harris:

From: Mark Harris, mh@mw.co.uk
Sent: 27th July 2015
Subject: Factory

Welcome back from your annual leave – just thought I'd update you on what's going on.

To put you in the picture I completed on the purchase of the factory last week and we are now in a position to fit out the space ready to commence production. As you already know the factory itself cost £1,500,000 which has been paid for out the finance raised from a new bank loan. On top of that we have so far paid £700,000 for plant and equipment and £150,000 for professional fees out of our available cash. The rest of the plant and equipment (approximately £800,000) will need to be paid for. We are a profitable business and we should have enough cash to cover this, even if it means using our £250,000 overdraft facility temporarily.

The production manager expects that we will start production on 1 October and that we will make our first sales to the national animal feed distributer in the middle of October on 60 day credit terms. We currently have 30 day credit terms with our suppliers.

Mark Harris
Director
MW
E: mh@mw.co.uk
T: 0151 266 3114

As a result of the email that you received on 27 July 2015, Mr Harris asked you to prepare a cash flow forecast for the next five months. You ascertain that on 1 August 2015, the balance in the bank was £400,000. You completed the cash forecast on 3 August 2015 and sent it to Mr Harris.

Your forecast can be accessed using the reference materials.

Exhibit 7 – Cash flow

Cash forecast for MW:

	August £100	September £100	October £100	November £100	December £100
Cash from receivables	382	395	405	405	740
Cash paid					
Payables	(212)	(262)	(358)	(365)	(350)
Other expenses	(80)	(90)	(110)	(110)	(110)
Plant and equipment	–	(600)	(200)	–	–
Dividend	–	(150)		–	–
Net cash flow	**90**	**(707)**	**(263)**	**(70)**	**280**
Cash balance b/fwd	400	490	(217)	(480)	(550)
Cash balance c/fwd	490	(217)	(480)	(550)	(270)

Exhibit 8 – Task

Upon receipt of the cash flow forecast Mr Harris becomes concerned and sends you the following email to which you need to respond.

From: Mark Harris, mh@mw.co.uk
Sent: 4th August 2015, 11:26 a.m.
Subject: Cash flow forecast and marketing

Thank you for the cash flow forecast that you sent through to me. I am a little alarmed and perplexed though that the forecast seems to show that we will breach our overdraft facility limit. Firstly, why is the position so bad? Secondly is there anything that we can do to improve the cash position so that the overdraft limit isn't breached?

On a related matter, given this cash position the effective marketing of our products is becoming a major consideration, in that we need to ensure that the new factory is utilised to near it's full capacity. In order to effectively market our products I've heard from a friend that we need to engage in business to business marketing, and perhaps employ a key account manager although I'm not clear how this differs from any other type of marketing. Please can you advise how this might help the business?

Thank you
Mark Harris
Director
MW
E: mh@mw.co.uk
T: 0151 266 3114

---

3 Summary

This chapter has introduced you to the unseen information for the pilot exam.

Next steps:

(1) You should work through this exam using the unseen information (ideally the online PearsonVue version) and the following chapter which contains lots of guidance to help you with your first attempt. The examiners consider it crucial that any practice you do, such as the pilot paper, is treated like an exam. You should therefore be writing out your own answers before reviewing the suggested solutions. Merely reading the requirements and then the suggested solutions has limited value.

Pilot exam – walkthrough

Chapter learning objectives

- To gain experience trying to answer a case study exam.

1 The aim of a walkthrough

The aim of this chapter is to give you a chance to practise many of the techniques you have been shown in previous chapters of this study text. This should help you to understand the various thought processes needed to complete the full three hour examination. It is important that you work through this chapter at a steady pace.

Don't rush on to the next stage until you have properly digested the information, followed the guidance labelled 'Stop and Think!' and made your own notes. This will give you more confidence than simply reading the model solutions. You should refer to the unseen produced in the previous chapter as you proceed through these exercises.

The following chapter will then guide you through the suggested solutions and marking key.

2 Summary of trigger 1

Two new products are being launched and will initially be using spare factory capacity. Mr Harris is currently negotiating with the first possible customer. MW is currently using simple absorption costing using direct labour hours and is considering a move to Activity Based Costing (ABC). A schedule of calculations has been prepared and sent to Mr Harris.

Stop and think!

(1) You won't need to do any calculations as they have already been done.

(2) Start thinking about the relevant information in the pre-seen. It's very important that your responses are applied to the scenario.

3 Overview of task 1

You need to prepare a report which covers:

• Differences between absorption costing and ABC.

• Advantages and disadvantages of ABC for MW.

• Implications for costing information.

• Difficulties when switching.

Let's plan

We need to create a planning page that ensures you identify and respond to all parts of the requirement. You can use the techniques discussed in Chapter eight or develop your own method. Here we will use the ordered list approach.

Split your planning sheet (use your wipe clean whiteboard) into a grid to ensure all four parts are covered:

Differences	Pros/cons of ABC for MW
Implications	Difficulties when switching

Note that each box is roughly the same size as we are assuming that each main task heading is equally weighted.

You now need to brainstorm all the relevant points you can think of under the above headings, making sure you are bringing together your knowledge from the relevant syllabus as well as your analysis of the pre-seen information.

Let's think a bit more about these requirements by breaking them down into the component parts.

'Differences between absorption costing and ABC' requires you to think about how each system works and therefore how they differ. It is useful to consider each process as a series of stages and consider whether each stage is the same or different in each system.

'Advantages and disadvantages of ABC' should be something quite familiar to you from your P1 studies. Although you may have loads of ideas here try to remember that this is just one task of four you need to complete in 45 minutes so avoid the temptation to go overboard. In 45 minutes you can be expected to explain approximately 25 ideas and so you should aim for about six points here – roughly three advantages and three disadvantages. Thought also needs to go into which points from your studies you decide to include. So for example it is not really appropriate here to discuss ABC in complex environments or service industries as neither of these points will be relevant to MW.

In order to respond the requirement on 'Implications for costing information' it is crucial that you use the information you have been given (in the additional reference materials) rather than just giving a general response.

Finally you need to consider the practicalities of this change for the final requirement looking at the difficulties which may be encountered. Again it is important to think about the nature of the MW business, the staff who may be affected, the systems which currently exist, amongst other issues.

As a rough rule of thumb you should spend about 15–20% of the time available for reading and planning. So for this section of the exam, where you are given 45 minutes, you should be spending approximately 7–8 minutes planning your answer before you complete the exercise below. This would leave you about 35 minutes to write your answer and a few minutes spare to check through what you have written.

Exercise 1

Prepare a response to the first task in the pilot exam MW.

4 Summary of trigger 2

MW needs to consider expansion to meet increasing demand. There is an opportunity to acquire the adjacent factory. There will be a need to consider how to recruit additional staff. Information is also given regarding the costs involved in investing in the new factory.

Stop and think!

(1) Think about your own experiences of recruitment to generate some ideas.

(2) Can you remember the financial reporting rules for capitalising an asset?

5 Summary of task 2

Respond to the email requesting:

- Advise whether online recruitment is suitable for this large scale recruitment and suggest other methods of recruitment for MW.

- How will the new property affect the financial statements now and profit in the future?

Let's plan

You can use the method of planning shown above or refer to Chapter 8 and use a mind map instead. The important thing is to generate some ideas and get the main points in some order before you start to write.

When you are discussing online recruitment think about how it might work at MW rather than just a general list of points. You need to make sure you leave adequate time to address any alternative recruitment options you think may be appropriate. You can think of your own experiences here and consider how recruitment is done at your company but make sure you keep your answers relevant to MW.

If you are struggling to think of how the asset will affect the financial statements it might be useful to work through (in your head) the main lines in the statement of financial position and statement of profit and loss and think about how they might be affected as well as considering how each number given in the task will be reflected in the financial statements. It is worth thinking about the relevant headings from IAS16 – i.e. initial recognition, subsequent measurement, subsequent expenditure, valuation and impairment.

Now spend 7–8 minutes completing your plan before attempting Exercise 2. You would then have 35 minutes to write your answer and a few minutes to check through what you have written before reviewing the solution.

Exercise 2

Prepare a response to the second task in the pilot exam MW.

6 Summary of trigger 3

Mr Harris is considering the need for a more formal budgeting system and wants guidance on the advantages of this as well as some information on the different approaches to setting budgets and also the types of individual budget which may be useful including information which may be needed.

Stop and think!

- Have you identified the THREE separate requirements here?

- Are you clear about the difference between approaches to setting budgets (e.g. zero based) and the types of individual budget (e.g. sales and production budgets)?

7 Summary of task 3

Respond to the email request for information.

Let's plan

You can use either method of planning here as long as you address all parts of the requirement. Make sure you note what is required carefully – for example you are asked to look at the benefits of budgets but not the problems. There will be no marks available for points that don't address the question set. Also ensure you leave enough time to consider the information needed to prepare the individual budgets – as there are a few easy marks available here.

Give yourself about 7–8 minutes to plan and then you can attempt exercise 3. You will then have about 35 minutes to write your answer, leaving a short amount of time to check through what you have written.

Exercise 3

Prepare a response to the third task in the pilot exam MW.

8 Summary of trigger 4

You are given some information regarding various costs and cash flows for MW. Additional reference materials show a cash flow forecast that you have recently prepared which suggests the overdraft limit will be breached.

Stop and think!

- What are the implications of breaching the overdraft?
- What other implications are there for MW of a poor cash position?
- Consider the reasons why this position has been forecast.

9 Summary of task 4

Respond to the email from Mr Harris requesting:

- An explanation for why the cash position appears to be so bad.
- What can be done to improve the position.
- An explanation of how business to business marketing and key account managers may help the company.

Let's plan

The best starting point here is to carry out a line by line review of the prepared forecast to identify first of all possible one-off items that may have caused the cash flow problem and secondly areas where improvements can be made. Also take a step back and consider more general cost savings which MW could implement in order to better control cash flow.

When considering the marketing requirement it is essential, as always, to tailor your response to MW rather than produce a generic and largely irrelevant response.

Exercise 4

Prepare a response to the fourth task in the pilot exam MW.

10 Summary

You should now have a better understanding of how to approach the exam requirements and plan your answer. Although this chapter uses the pilot exam as an example, the techniques used can be applied to any set of exam tasks.

Next steps:

(1) As previously mentioned, you should attempt a written answer yourself to all of the tasks before reviewing the suggested solutions.

(2) Reviewing the solutions may highlight knowledge gaps which you may need to revisit.

Test your understanding answers

Exercise 1

> *These answers have been provided by CIMA for information purposes only. The answers created are indicative of a response that could be given by a good candidate. They are not to be considered exhaustive, and other appropriate relevant responses would receive credit.*
>
> *CIMA will not accept challenges to these answers on the basis of academic judgement.*

Section 1:

Report to Mr Harris and Mr Webb

Re: Possible change from traditional absorption costing to activity based costing

Purpose of report:

This report will cover the following:

- How an activity based costing (ABC) system differs from a traditional absorption costing system.

- The advantages and disadvantages to MW of using ABC.

- The implications of using ABC on MW's costing information.

- The potential difficulties we might face in changing to activity based costing.

How ABC differs from a traditional absorption costing system

The key difference between an ABC system and an absorption costing system is the way in which the fixed overhead cost is included within the standard cost per bag of product. It is important to note that the treatment of direct material, direct labour and variable overhead is the same in both.

At the moment, under absorption costing total fixed overheads and total labour hours are estimated at the start of the year and these are used to calculate an absorption rate for fixed overhead on a per direct labour hour basis. This is then applied to CHICKEN and SHEEP on the basis of the number of direct labour hours that each product uses to establish the fixed overhead cost per bag. Therefore under absorption costing we assume that there is a direct link between the overhead being incurred and the amount of direct hours used in production, in other words that production overhead costs are driven by the direct labour hours used in production.

Under ABC, instead of assuming that overhead costs are driven by direct labour hours, there is an assumption that costs are driven by activities which are known as cost drivers. For each activity or cost driver there will be a cost pool which is simply the total overhead cost generated by that activity.

As you can see from the costing schedule, in the case of MW the following cost pools have been identified – machinery set up costs, ingredients handling costs and inspection costs – as these have been identified as the key activities that generate overhead cost within our production processes. Any overhead cost that doesn't fit into one of these categories is included in other overhead. Therefore a key difference between the two systems is the way in which the actual cost information is collated and in the case of ABC broken down.

Another key difference is the way in which the total costs within these cost pools is absorbed into a unit of production. Under absorption costing total direct labour hours are used to establish an overhead absorption rate which is then used to work out the overhead cost per bag based upon the number of hours taken to produce one bag. ABC on the other hand uses the total number of activities within each cost pool to calculate an overhead absorption rate per activity for each separate cost pool.

In MW's case the activities will be number of set ups (for machinery set up costs), number of ingredients movements (for ingredient handling costs) and number of inspections (for inspection costs). The overhead cost per bag of each product is then calculated by multiplying the rate per activity with the number of activities for one bag of production.

Advantages and disadvantages for MW of using ABC:

Advantages:

ABC is likely to give us a more accurate cost per bag because our four products, being of different sizes and with different production volumes, will utilise or use overhead at different rates. This in turn means that pricing of CHICKEN, SHEEP, HORSE and GOAT will be more accurate and management decision making more meaningful.

By setting up ABC you will be able to understand more fully what drives overhead costs. By understanding the drivers of cost, we will be better placed to react and control costs.

ABC recognises that not all overhead costs are driven by production or sales volumes.

Disadvantages:

The application of ABC can be more time consuming and therefore costly because of the level of detail required. Care needs to be taken that the benefit from using it (that is, the more useful information as identified above) is not outweighed by this cost. Where production is simple and products are limited such as in our case then ABC is unlikely to be beneficial overall.

Not all overhead costs can be allocated to activity cost pools and therefore there will also be an element of overhead absorbed on a traditional basis.

Implications of using ABC on our costing information:

The application of ABC to the absorption of overheads means that more overhead is allocated to HORSE and GOAT and less to SHEEP (the difference in CHICKEN is negligible). This is because production of HORSE and GOAT must generate a greater proportion of the cost drivers. This is likely to be because as new products they will be sold and therefore produced in relatively small batches which will require a greater proportion of set ups. Additionally HORSE and GOAT have greater material content than CHICKEN and SHEEP and therefore will have generated a greater proportion of the ingredient handling costs.

The costing schedules show that if pricing decisions were based on absorption costing that potentially HORSE would be sold for less than its activity based cost. This could potentially lead to an erosion of MW's margins and therefore potentially the use of ABC will be beneficial to MW.

The costing statement for ABC shows that a significant proportion of overheads will still be allocated on a direct labour hour basis, although it's possible with more time to look into identifying cost pools and activities that this could be reduced.

Potential difficulties of changing to ABC:

The potential difficulties of changing to an activity based costing approach will include:

- Determining the cost drivers and cost pools based on real data rather than estimated data.
- Budgeting the costs for each cost pool.
- Ensuring that information can be captured regarding the usage of these cost drivers for each product.
- ABC would become more complex and timely to manage as the number of products grows in the business.

Exercise 2

Email to Mr Harris:

To: Mr Harris
From: Candidate
Date: 24 June 2015

Hello Mr Harris,

Please see below my responses to your requests for information.

Recruitment

Decisions need to be made about the sources from which to recruit, at what cost and by which media. We also need to have a clear idea of the range of skills we are seeking to recruit, the level of experience, technical ability and salary we are prepared to offer.

Achieving the correct balance of response is essential as if the process generates too few applications, or too many that are unsuitable it can become very costly and time consuming.

Having given due consideration to these requirements we can use closed searches and responsive methods such as:

- Speculative applications/word of mouth, we can make our existing staff aware of the possible vacancies through the use of notice boards and asking if they are aware of anyone who may be interested.

- Links to schools, colleges and universities, will require some organisation and time with presentations to students at jobs fairs.

- Recruitment agencies, which may be useful for the recruitment of broad based skills.

- Search consultants, may be useful for specific skill requirements but may be the most expensive option.

- Or open searches.

- Local and national newspaper adverts, which can be costly and may not attract the required applicants.

- Adverts in the specialist press, more likely to succeed at identifying our skill requirements but more costly than general advertising.

- Employment centre adverts, cheaper will possibly produce unfocussed results.

- The organisation's website, although time will be needed to formulate the recruitment section, relatively cheap and will give wide coverage.

- Radio and TV adverts, these are relatively expensive and may produce unfocussed results.

As you have heard, the use of the organisation website as a means of recruitment has been growing in popularity both as a result of easy access and low cost, with more than 78% of organisations now potentially recruiting by this means.

Advantages to MW

Reduced costs of recruitment, apart from design costs of adverts, which we may be able to achieve in house, coverage on the internet is very cost effective.

Improved organisation image if website is well designed, this is an opportunity to explain fully that we are a growing company, with good future prospects.

Reduced administration, once on the web very little maintenance should be required.

Shorter recruitment cycle, the response time will be reduced, but important here to specify the requirements accurately, and filter early in the process.

Wider pool of applicants, including overseas candidates can be expected to apply, thus enhancing the likelihood of finding required skills.

Easier process for candidates to complete, it is relatively simple to apply on-line.

Disadvantages to MW

Too many unsuitable applicants, because of the relative ease and speed mentioned above, the process may attract many unsuitable applications which will take time to review.

Technical problems with the website, it is important that the website is technically functional.

Not enough information about the position or organisation, care needed with this when designing the adverts which need to contain sufficient background information about MW.

The impersonal nature of the process, it is important to make the web site as user friendly as possible, MW must look like a pleasant place to work.

Poorly designed website may deter applicants and give them the wrong impression about MW and our ethos.

Given the various pro and cons a balanced approach of both broad website campaign associated with some more focussed closed search methods should be adopted to enable us to recruit the required skills at reasonable cost.

Impact of the acquisition of property on the future financial statements and profit of MW

IAS 16 Property, plant and equipment is the international financial reporting standard which governs the accounting treatment of property in the financial statements.

Initial recognition:

The property will be initially recognised at cost in the statement of financial position as a non-current asset as long as it is probable that economic benefit will flow to MW and that the cost can be measured reliably (both of these criteria are clearly met here). The cost at which the property is initially recognised will include its purchase price but also any associated professional fees. Therefore the property will have an initial value of $1,650,000, which will increase non-current assets in the statement of financial position.

Subsequent measurement:

In accordance with IAS 16, subsequent to initial recognition the property will be subject to a depreciation charge which will reduce profit much in the same way that we depreciate the plant and equipment that we currently own. One difference will be however that the property is likely to have an estimated life significantly longer than existing plant and equipment and therefore the depreciation rate will be lower.

In order to calculate the depreciable amount of the property, the land and building elements of the property need to be split as under IAS 16 land is not depreciated. We know that land is valued at £500,000 at purchase and therefore the element of the £1,650,000 that would not be depreciated would be £550,000 (= £500,000 + ((£500,000/£1,500,000) × £150,000). Therefore the building element of the property has a cost of £1,100,000. To arrive at depreciable amount however we will need to make an assessment of any residual value and net this off. We will also need to make an assessment of useful life as well in order to calculate the depreciation.

There are a few additional points to make in respect of IAS 16 and property in respect of any subsequent expenditure, valuation and impairment.

Subsequent expenditure:

If in the future we incur additional costs in respect of the property then as long as this expenditure improves the future economic benefits that the property will generate then it can capitalised and included as part of the asset value in the statement of financial position. If however, the expenditure relates to general maintenance then it will need to be treated as an expense which will reduce profit in the future.

Valuation

Under IAS 16 there is a choice of accounting policy regarding the carrying value of assets. It is possible the property could be annually re-valued to its market value. If this policy is chosen then any revaluation movement will be shown in reserves rather than impacting on profit.

Impairment

In accordance with IAS 36 Impairment of Assets, all assets of an entity need to be reviewed for indications of impairment annually (where impairment is defined as occurring when the carrying value of an asset is greater than its recoverable amount). Such an impairment might occur to the property value if its market value were to decline markedly. This could then potentially reduce profit in the future.

Please let me know if you need any further information.

Kind regards

Candidate

Exercise 3

Section 3

Email to Mr Harris:

To: Mr Harris
From: Candidate
Date: 1 July 2015

RE: Budgeting queries:

The benefits of setting more formal budgets:

There would be many benefits to MW of setting up and using formal budgets which include:

Planning:

By setting detailed budgets it forces us as a management team to plan ahead and to take time out to complete the budget process. It will allow us to look into the long term as well as focusing on the short term.

Control and evaluation:

The budget gives a benchmark against which to compare the actual results. Variance reports of the difference between budgeted and actual results can be produced which can be used to hold staff to account for inefficiencies and overspends. Such reports will also allow us to set more realistic budgets in the future which could have a knock on impact on product costing and pricing.

Co-ordination:

A more formal budget allows for the different parts of the business to be reconciled to each other. This will become increasingly important as the business expands as we might need to set up different departments to deal with sales, production and distribution. A formal plan or budget will allow each department to work together.

Communication:

Budgets can be used to communicate targets to all staff within the business. Again this is going to be increasingly important with the business expanding. We cannot expect staff to work efficiently if they are unaware of the overall plan.

The different approaches to budget setting and their appropriateness to MW:

The following are approaches that can be adopted when setting budgets:

Incremental budgeting:

This approach is where the previous year's budget is used as a base, with incremental changes made to reflect known movements in costs, prices and other factors. This is clearly not appropriate to MW for the first year but could be used once budgets are embedded as long as MW doesn't change too much in terms of number of products and scale of production.

Zero-based budgeting

As the name suggests this approach treats the budget as a new event every year and starts the process from scratch. This forces management to re-evaluate all of the activities of the business each time a budget is set. This is likely to be the most appropriate approach for MW to take if significant expansion occurs or a large range of new products are developed.

Activity-based budgeting:

Activity based budgeting is similar to activity based costing in that it is a budget based around an activity framework. In effect an activity based budget is one where a budget is set for each of the cost pools within an activity based costing system – therefore it is only appropriate where such a costing system is used.

Types of individual budget:

The master budget is in effect the end product of the budget process and will contain:

- Budgeted statement of profit or loss.
- Cash budget.
- Capital expenditure budget.
- Budgeted statement of financial position.

In order to arrive at this a series of individual budgets will be needed which ultimately build upon each other. Examples of individual budgets and the information required to complete them are shown below:

Sales budget

- Quantity (number of bags) of each product (that is CHICKEN, SHEEP, HORSE and GOAT) expected to be sold in the year.

- Expected selling price per bag of product.

Production budget

- Number of bags in opening inventory of CHICKEN, SHEEP, HORSE and GOAT.

- Sales (from the sales budget).

- Planned closing inventory in number of bags of each product.

- Sales + closing inventory – opening inventory gives production in terms of bags.

Ingredient requirement budget

- Opening inventory of all types of ingredient used in production in kg.

- Number of kg of each ingredient required for production – using CHICKEN as an example, for each ingredient used the quantity used in production will be found by multiplying the number of kg per unit of CHICKEN by the number of CHICKEN to be produced (from the production budget).

- Planned closing inventory in kg of each type of ingredient.

- Production + closing inventory – opening inventory gives purchases.

Ingredient purchase cost budget

- Purchases of each ingredient from the ingredient requirement budget.

- Price per kg of each ingredient.

- Purchases × cost per kg gives ingredient cost.

Exercise 4

Section 4:

To: Mr Harris
From: Candidate
Date: 4 August 2015

Hello Mr Harris

Please find below my response to your email.

Why the overdraft position is so bad:

I agree that on first sight the overdraft does appear to be alarming. However, there are a number of specific reasons for this and we should not be worried that this is a permanent position because it is likely that had January been included that you would have seen MW returning to a positive cash balance.

The reasons for the overdraft and why it worsens are:

(1) Production in the new factory will start on 1 October which means that ingredients need to be purchased in advance of this. From the forecast we can see that cash paid to payables increases significantly from October which reflects these purchases.

(2) Other expenses (which will include labour costs) will also increase from October as production commences.

(3) The first sales receipts from this production, however, will not materialise until December because these sales are made on 60 day credit terms. Indeed December will be the first month of "normal" cash flow and as you can see a positive inflow will be generated.

(4) The purchase of £800,000 for plant and equipment will clearly have an impact on cash flow.

(5) The dividend to be paid in September is also a factor.

Measures that MW could take to improve the overdraft position:

(1) The dividend could be delayed by three months. This will clearly depend upon your need for the cash as you are the main shareholder.

(2) Whilst the plant and equipment needs to be purchased in order for the factory to become operational, it might be possible to lease the assets rather than acquire them outright. This will have the benefit of spreading the cash flow over the life of the asset.

(3) We could seek to negotiate different payment terms with both suppliers and the new customer. It would be advisable to have both on the same terms.

(4) We could tighten up on production and ensure that we only order ingredients when required and therefore reduce our levels on inventory.

(5) We could take out another loan to support the working capital investment needed for the new factory.

Marketing:

A key aspect with regard to marketing is that the customers of MW are businesses in their own right, some key points regarding the differences between B2B and consumer marketing is as follows:

(1) The intended customer is an organisation rather than an individual; as such you have been the organisational face of MW, dealing with our present customers, many of whom were individual farmers in the early days of the business. With the growth of MW and the expansion of our customer base to include larger organisations we are now dealing with their buyers on a business to business basis.

(2) These organisations buy and use our products to support their organisational objectives, different marketing programmes are required to reach and influence organisational buyers, explaining how our products can assist them in achieving these objectives, for example the unique nutritional value of our products enabling them to produce healthier livestock faster.

(3) In the business sector our customers buy a range of products and services to either make new products or enable production processes to operate successfully, and as such it is important for us to understand their business objectives and show how we can help them achieve these. As mentioned above healthier higher value livestock can be produced.

(4) Businesses will use defined processes and procedures to buy products and services and the decisions attached to securing the necessary products will be controlled by a small number of people, the 'buyers' in these organisations This is unlike consumer–based marketing where decisions often involve a large number of people. It is in our interests for our future key account manager to know them and understand their requirements.

(5) Even though there may be several people associated with a buying decision in an organisation, the overall number of people involved is very small compared to the millions of people involved in everyday purchases such as chocolates.

(6) The financial value of organisational purchase orders will be much larger and the frequency much lower, as such it is in our interests to maintain close contact with our customers, monitoring purchases, maintaining contact with them to indicate our interest.

(7) Given the size of orders and the requirements for consistent quality, agreements may be made between organisations for the supply of materials over a number of years, and consequently we must be prepared for the negotiation processes to be lengthy.

Although there are differences many of the characteristics of the consumer decision making process can still be observed in the organisational context.

Organisational buyers (our customers) make decisions which ultimately contribute to the achievement of our corporate objectives. To make the necessary decisions a high volume of pertinent information is required, which needs to be detailed and presented in a rational and logical style.

This puts the organisational buyer in a very important role. It is essential that those liaising understand these concepts, and as such the role and importance of the key account manager in building trusting relationships with such individuals cannot be understated.

It is vitally important that we fully understand our customers, have good relationships with their key staff, and convince them that our products can help them achieve their business objectives. As such an effective key account manager will be a necessary addition to our skill base in the near future.

Pilot exam – understanding the solution and marking guide

Chapter learning objectives

- To gain a deeper understanding of the marking guide and learn how to write an answer that scores well.

1 Introduction

As we have already explained in previous chapters the case study examinations are marked against a series of competencies. It is important that you understand this process to ensure you maximise your marks in the exam.

Once you have reviewed Chapter ten, attempted the exercises and reviewed the suggested solutions this chapter takes you through the detail of how these exercises would be marked. We have also a sample student script to show some possible strengths and weaknesses which you may recognise in your own answer.

Note: The CIMA official marking guide for the pilot case is given as follows:

Competency	Section/task	Marks	Total marks available for competency
Technical skills	(1) ABC vs traditional costing	21	64
	(2) Impact of new factory on finance statements	11	
	(3) Budgeting queries	23	
	(4) Cash position	7	
	Integration	2	
Business skills	(2) Impact of new factory on recruitment	6	16
	(3) Budgeting queries	2	
	(4) Marketing	7	
	Integration	1	
People skills	(1) ABC vs traditional costing	4	14
	(2) Impact of new factory on recruitment	6	
	(4) Marketing	4	
Leadership skills	(4) Cash position	6	6

In this chapter we try to show how these marks could have been awarded/won.

2 Exam section 1

As we saw in the previous chapter the first section you were required to prepare a report covering:

- Differences between absorption costing and ABC
- Advantages and disadvantages of ABC for MW
- Implications for costing information
- Difficulties when switching

The overall marking grid given above can be translated into more detail for task 1 as follows:

TASK 1		Technical skills	Business skills	People skills	Leadership skills
How ABC differs from traditional:					
Difference relates to how fixed overhead is included in standard cost per unit		1			
Cost drivers (including examples appropriate to MW)	Up to	4			
Cost pools based on activity (including examples appropriate to MW)	Up to	4			
Advantages and disadvantages:					
More accurate costing per unit	Up to	2			
Understand what drives costs	Up to	2			
Time consuming and costly to set up and monitor	Up to	2			
Not all costs can be linked to drivers	Up to	2			

Implications of using ABC on the costing information:					
Analysis of costing schedule (recognise that products with greatest material content have the greatest share of the overhead)	Up to	4			
Implications for pricing and margins (decision making and communication)	Up to			5	
Potential difficulties:					
Determining cost drivers and cost pools	Up to	2			
Determining budgeted costs	Up to	2			
Sophistication of information gathering	Up to	2			
Costs of setting up and monitoring	Up to	2			
Potential available marks		29		5	
Maximum that would be awarded		21		4	

Note that in many cases the grid specifies "up to..." This is partly to reflect the fact that there are a range of possible points that could be made but also that extra marks could be awarded if a point is developed further.

To see how this works, let us now discuss the model answer to task 1.

Differences between absorption costing and ABC

This whole section is allocated 45 minutes so for each part of the exercise you have approximately 11 minutes. Working on a rough ratio of 2 minutes for every point you make, this implies you need to make about 5–6 points. At this level you are looking at earning up to 2 marks per point where that is developed, but you should avoid going into unnecessary detail.

- The first short section is just a brief overview of what the report will cover and doesn't score any marks directly. As such, it could be avoided if you feel time is going to be tight.

However, an introduction can earn marks if it applies the wider context to the organisation concerned. For example, here we could have commented that many small organisations such as MW make the switch from traditional overhead absorption to ABC once they extend their product ranges.

- The answer then goes straight into the key differences starting with

"... is the way in which the fixed overhead cost is included within the standard cost per bag of product."

This is not enough to earn marks on its own but is an important starting point which can be built on by explaining how fixed overhead is included under each method.

- The key points regarding absorption costing are then explained including

"total fixed overheads and total labour hours are estimated at the start of the year and these are used to calculate an absorption rate".

This will earn a mark followed by another mark for further explanation.

"under absorption costing we assume that there is a direct link between the overhead being incurred and the amount of direct hours used in production".

- The answer then goes on to explain that

"Under ABC, instead of assuming that overhead costs are driven by direct labour hours, there is an assumption that costs are driven by activities which are known as cost drivers."

As this is comparing absorption costing with ABC, rather than just describing them, this will earn a mark.

- Do ensure you are aiming to apply your response to the scenario wherever possible. So the answer then states

  "in the case of MW the following cost pools have been identified – machinery set up costs, ingredients handling costs and inspection costs – as these have been identified as the key activities that generate overhead cost within our production processes".

  This uses MW to illustrate a point made about cost pools in the previous paragraph and so will earn a mark.

- Note that the suggested solution makes it very clear when a relevant point has been made by using appropriate **language**. So the next sentence which refers to the way in which overheads are allocated explains

  "a key difference between the two systems is the way in which the actual cost information is collated and in the case of ABC broken down".

  The use of the terms identified in the requirement (i.e. 'key difference') will show the marker you are still on track and serves as a good reminder to yourself that this is the topic you are discussing. This point highlighted above will also earn a mark.

  This technique continues in the next paragraph with the following point earning another mark.

  "Another key difference is the way in which the total costs within these cost pools is absorbed into a unit of production."

  This is then explained in the context of MW.

You may have noticed there are more than six marks identified above. This is typical of a case study exam which will often have various possible responses and therefore more marks available than the maximum you can score.

Advantages and disadvantages of ABC for MW

You may well have learned a whole list of advantages and disadvantages of ABC but the important thing here is to **APPLY** every point you make to MW.

- Here are some examples of how to do this from the model solution:

"ABC is likely to give us a more accurate cost per bag because our four products, being of different sizes and with different production volumes, will utilise or use overhead at different rates"

"pricing of CHICKEN, SHEEP, HORSE and GOAT will be more accurate"

"Where production is simple and products are limited such as in our case then ABC is unlikely to be beneficial overall"

Implications for costing information

It is important here to ensure you use the information provided in the schedule.

- The answer begins with an overview of the situation by stating:

"The application of ABC to the absorption of overheads means that more overhead is allocated to HORSE and GOAT and less to SHEEP (the difference in CHICKEN is negligible). This is because production of HORSE and GOAT must generate a greater proportion of the cost drivers."

This is applied well to the scenario and earns a mark.

- You could explain this point further by considering the reasons behind the difference, thus earning another mark:

"This is likely to be because as new products they will be sold and therefore produced in relatively small batches which will require a greater proportion of set ups"

This illustrates how useful it is to bear in mind that sometimes you can earn more than one mark from a point by considering, in more detail, how it applies to the scenario.

- Additional marks are available for this requirement with the following points:

  "The costing schedules show that if pricing decisions were based on absorption costing that potentially HORSE would be sold for less than its activity based cost"

  This is further explained:

  "This could potentially lead to an erosion of MW's margins and therefore potentially the use of ABC will be beneficial to MW",

  thus earning a further mark.

- And finally:

  "The costing statement for ABC shows that a significant proportion of overheads will still be allocated on a direct labour hour basis, although it's possible with more time to look into identifying cost pools and activities that this could be reduced."

Difficulties when switching to ABC

You can see the model solution gives a fairly brief response to the fourth requirement. We suggest you begin with the assumption that each part of a task is worth an equal number of marks. However it is possible that when you are planning your answer you struggle to identify an equal number of points for each part of the task. If this happens don't panic! Just make sure you make a reasonable attempt at each part and move on.

- Although we have only earned four marks with the following points, we have already earned sufficient credit with the previous requirements to score maximum marks in this section.

  "Determining the cost drivers and cost pools based on real data rather than estimated data."

  "Budgeting the costs for each cost pool."

  "Ensuring that information can be captured regarding the usage of these cost drivers for each product."

  "ABC would become more complex and timely to manage as the number of products grows in the business."

Note: While some students find model answers inspiring as something to aspire to, others prefer to see a script that would have passed but is closer to what most students would be producing within the time constraints given. The following illustration shows such a script.

While neither covering as may areas nor developing points as much as in the model solution, this answer would still have scored a strong pass. Note in particular how most of the comments made have been applied to MW.

Section 1:

Report to Mr Harris and Mr Webb

Re: Possible change from traditional absorption costing to activity based costing

Introduction

This report will cover how activity based costing (ABC) differs from traditional absorption costing system, the pros and cons of each and how a switch could affect MW.

How ABC differs from a traditional absorption costing system

Both ABC and absorption costing look at how fixed overheads are included within the standard cost per bag of product.

At the moment, under absorption costing, all fixed overheads are absorbed on a single direct labour hour basis. For example, because a bag of CHICKEN takes 25% less time to produce than SHEEP, it will be given 25% less fixed overhead cost per bag. For this to make sense, it assumes that production overhead costs are linked to, or driven by, the direct labour hours used in production. Under ABC, this assumption is challenged.

With ABC overheads are split into different cost pools with the idea that each pool can have a different cost driver that better reflects how those costs are generated and that can be used to absorb overheads.

For MW the following cost pools and drivers have been identified:

- set up costs – driven by the number of set ups,

- handling costs – driven by the number of movements and

- inspection costs – driven by the number of inspections.

Any overheads that don't fit into one of these categories are absorbed using the traditional approach of labour hours.

Advantages and disadvantages for MW of using ABC:

Advantages:

Because we are looking at fixed overheads, it could be argued that any method of absorbing costs is arbitrary. However, by using a range of cost drivers that more closely model how costs are generated, ABC is likely to give us a more accurate cost per bag making pricing and other decisions better.

For example, HORSE and GOAT have greater material content than CHICKEN and SHEEP, so will have generated a greater proportion of ingredient handling movements and so should be given a greater share of the handling costs.

Also, by setting up ABC, you will be able to understand more fully what drives overhead costs and be better placed to control costs. For example, is there a more efficient way of carrying out inspections to reduce the number of inspections required?

Disadvantages:

The application of ABC can be more time consuming and therefore costly because of the level of detail required.

MW has only four products and a simple production process, so it is debatable whether a switch to ABC is likely to be beneficial overall.

Implications of using ABC on our costing information:

The greatest difference between traditional costing and ABC is with HORSE, where the ABC cost is significantly higher. The danger here is that a price for HORSE set using traditional absorption costing may be too low.

Potential difficulties of changing to ABC:

The potential difficulties of changing to ABC include:

* Identifying the cost drivers and cost pools.

* Measuring cost driver volumes.

* ABC is more complex and time consuming so staff will require training.

3 Exam section 2

From the previous chapter we saw that this section required the following:

- Advise whether online recruitment is suitable for this large scale recruitment and suggest other methods of recruitment for MW.

- How will the new property affect the financial statements now and profit in the future.

It is important to note for the below marking guide and those that follow that they represent a comprehensive answer which contains sufficient points to earn more than maximum marks. There may also be other points which are not made here which would also earn credit. Also note that each point would need to be explained sufficiently – the few words given here are unlikely to earn full credit and you should refer to the model solutions in Chapter 10 for the detailed answers.

TASK 2		Technical skills	Business skills	People skills	Leadership skills
Effectiveness of on-line recruitment:					
Time and cost implications	Up to		2		
Wider applicant base	Up to		2		
Impact on corporate image	Up to		2		
Technical difficulties	Up to		2		
Alternative recruitment sources:					
Speculative	Up to			2	
Job fairs	Up to			2	
Adverts	Up to			2	
Consultants	Up to			2	

Impact of new factory on financial statements:					
Initial recognition at cost as a non current asset		1			
Professional fees capitalised (including calc)	Up to	2			
Subsequent measurement:					
– Land		1			
– Depreciation (incl calc of depreciable amount)	Up to	3			
– Subsequent expenditure	Up to	2			
– Revaluation/impairment	Up to	2			
– Impact on future profit	Up to	2			
Potential available marks		*13*	*8*	*8*	
Maximum that would be awarded		*11*	*6*	*6*	

Exercise 1 – Marking exercise

The following answer represents a possible student response to Section 2:

Suitability of online recruitment

Lots of companies use online recruitment. Online recruitment involves advertising the role online and also possibly gathering applications through an online portal. Large companies will have a very attractive section of the website devoted to recruitment which will have all the roles advertised as well as information about the company and benefits of working with them.

MW could use online recruitment to improve the efficiency of the recruitment process and therefore reduce costs. This would be particularly appropriate as there are likely to several new roles to fill when the new factory opens.

This method of recruitment would also be much quicker than any other method.

Using online recruitment would allow MW to reach a wider pool of applicants. This may be important as they are trying to recruit a relatively large number of staff from the same area and may not have sufficient word of mouth capabilities to reach enough potential recruits.

Using online recruitment is more dynamic so the advert and information can be easily amended if the situation changes, for example if a role is filled. This is not the case with other more static methods such as newspaper adverts.

One problem with online recruitment for MW is they are unlikely to have the relevant IT skills to create the website themselves and so there may be a cost involved.

Other recruitment methods

As MW is looking to recruit in the same area it could use its current workforce to help to advertise. They could use job boards in the offices and factory to make staff aware of the vacancies and maybe even offer incentives to staff if they introduce a new successful applicant. This may well be cheaper than other recruitment methods. There is a danger that staff will introduce lots of unsuitable candidates to try and earn the incentive and this could prove costly and take up lots of management time. Staff may also be upset if their introductions are not successful and may resent those who do get the job.

MW could use the job centre to assist in recruitment as this will attract a wide number of people. However this may then take time to sort through all of the applications.

Other methods include newspaper adverts.

Impact on financial statements

The property will initially be recognised at cost in the statement of financial position. Cost includes purchase price and associated professional fees.

The property will then be depreciated over the useful economic life of the asset. Depreciation will reduce the value of the asset and will also reduce profit each year. The amount depreciated will be reduced by the residual value of the asset (what it is likely to be worth at the end of its life).

If the property increases in value it can be revalued upwards in future years. This increase in value would be shown in reserves rather than profit.

If the property suffers a long term reduction in value it will have to be impaired. This involves reducing the value of the property but unlike an upwards revaluation this impairment will reduce profit. This is the principle of prudence.

Requirement:

Determine the likely marks awarded for this answer.

Remember that the marking guide is not rigid and any sensible and relevant point can score credit.

4 Exam section 3

This task required:

- advantages of a formal budgeting system
- different approaches to setting budgets
- types of individual budget which may be useful including information which may be needed.

TASK 3		Technical skills	Business skills	People skills	Leadership skills
Benefits of setting more formal budgets:					
Planning	Up to	2			
Control and evaluation	Up to	2			
Co-ordination	Up to	2			
Communication	Up to	2			
Different approaches to budget setting:					
Incremental budgeting	Up to	3			
Activity based budgeting	Up to	3			
Zero based budgeting	Up to	3			
Types of budget (incl info needed):					
Master budget	Up to	3			
Sales budget	Up to	3			
Production budget	Up to	3			
Ingredients budgets	Up to	3			
Potential available marks		29			
Maximum that would be awarded		25			

Illustrative script for task 3

> *Despite much of the answer lacking specific application to MW, this script would still have been a pass.*

Email to Mr Harris:

To: Mr Harris
From: Candidate
Date: 1 July 2015

RE: Budgeting queries:

The benefits of setting more formal budgets:

Planning:

Setting budgets forces MW to plan ahead allowing MW to anticipate and respond to trends rather than crisis management.

Control and evaluation:

Budgets gives a benchmark against which to compare the actual results, enabling better management control through variance analysis.

Co-ordination and communication:

Budgeting forces the different parts of the business to work together to come up with a common plan. This will become increasingly important as MW expands.

The different approaches to budget setting and their appropriateness to MW:

- *Incremental budgeting:*

  This approach is where adjustments are made to the previous year's budget, say to include price rises due to inflation. This is not appropriate to MW in the first year but could be used thereafter.

- *Zero-based budgeting:*

  ZBB starts the budget from scratch and all costs and activities have to be justified. This is likely to be best for MW if significant growth occurs or new products developed.

- *Activity-based budgeting:*

  Activity based budgeting is where a budget is set for each of the cost pools within an ABC system – therefore it is only useful if ABC is adopted.

Types of individual budget:

The master budget will contain a budgeted statement of profit or loss, a budgeted statement of financial position, a cash budget and a capital expenditure budget. To generate this a series of individual budgets will be needed – for example,

Sales budget

- Budgeted revenue = expected sales quantity (bags) × expected selling price
- Do this for each product (CHICKEN, SHEEP, HORSE and GOAT) and in total

Production budget

- Budgeted production in bags = (Sales volume + planned closing inventory – opening inventory)
- Do this for each product (CHICKEN, SHEEP, HORSE and GOAT)

Ingredient usage budget

- Budgeted usage of ingredients = budgeted production in bags for each product × number of kg of ingredient per bag

Ingredient purchase cost budget

- Budgeted purchases in kg = (amount required for production + planned closing inventory – opening inventory) for each ingredient
- Purchases = Budgeted purchases in kg × cost per kg for each ingredient

5 Exam section 4

This section requires:

- An explanation for why the cash position appears to be so bad
- What can be done to improve the position
- An explanation of how business to business marketing and key account managers may help the company.

TASK 4		Technical skills	Business skills	People skills	Leadership skills
Why the cash position is so bad:					
Impact of new factory on:					
– Inventory building	Up to	3			
– Receivables	Up to	3			
– Other costs	Up to	2			
– Recognition of timing of capex and dividend	Up to	2			
Measures to improve the overdraft position:					
Delay dividend	Up to				2
Change credit terms	Up to				2
Efficient production to reduce inventory	Up to				2
Lease assets	Up to				2
Take out a medium term loan to match with life of asset	Up to				2

Difference between B2B and consumer marketing:					
Up to 2 marks per issue	Up to		8		
Relevance of key account managers:	Up to			4	
Potential available marks		10	8	4	10
Maximum that would be awarded		7	7	4	6

Illustrative script for task 4

> *While much shorter than the model answer, this script manages to cover all the key areas required and so would have been a pass.*

To: Mr Harris
From: Candidate
Date: 4 August 2015

Hello Mr Harris

Why the overdraft position is so bad:

The reasons for the overdraft and why it worsens are:

Time delays

- Production in the new factory will start on 1 October but ingredients will need to be bought before this. Cash paid to suppliers for ingredients increases significantly from October.

- Because of a 60 day credit period, cash from customers for sales will not be received until December.

Large one-off payments

- Both the payment for plant and equipment and the dividend add to cash flow pressure.

Most of these are timing issues, rather than indicative of underlying problems and MW will return to a positive cash flow in December and a positive overall cash balance in January.

Measures that MW could take to improve the overdraft position:

(1) Delay the dividend by three months, assuming this does not cause you personal liquidity problems.

(2) Assuming such leases can be found, MW could lease the new plant and machinery rather than buying them outright. This will convert the upfront payment into a series of monthly payments.

(3) Depending on industry norms, MW could try to negotiate different payment terms with both suppliers and the new customer.

(4) Subject to the risks of inventory stock-outs, MW could order ingredients only when required to reduce levels of inventory.

Marketing:

As MW grows it will be dealing with more larger organisations rather than individual farmers. This has a number of implications for MW:

(1) Organisations buy products to support their own organisational objectives so MW's marketing efforts should focus on understanding and targeting these objectives. For example, the nutritional value of MW products could help a business produce healthier livestock faster.

(2) Organisations often have set processes and procedures to buy products, so MW will need to understand these processes, especially identifying key people who make the buying decisions, building relationships with them and understanding their needs. Having key account managers can help here.

(3) Organisations are more likely to enter into lengthy negotiations to then agree to longer term contracts. This may require MW to be able to supply large volumes of detailed information and have strong negotiation skills. Again a key account manager can fulfil such a role.

6 Integration

There are 3 integration marks available in the pilot paper with marks spread across each of the generic competencies.

These marks will be awarded for the overall quality of your answer and use of available information. You should consider the style and language you use and ensure it is suitable for the intended recipient. It is also important that your responses are appropriately structured and logical.

You need to ensure that you integrate relevant parts of each of the three technical syllabi to score well here – don't view a task as just covering one of the underlying papers. Instead look for opportunities to cover more than one paper at a time – for example, how could a production decision (P1) affect marketing (E1) and working capital (F1)?

7 Summary

You should now have an understanding of how the case studies are marked which is crucial if you are going to improve your performance. It is very important that you understand what will (and won't) earn credit in the exam.

Next steps:

(1) Revisit any chapters that you found tricky.

(2) Download the variant 2 exam based on the pilot case from the CIMA website, and work through the different tasks and triggers for additional practice.

(3) Continue with the following chapters which look at the February 2015 exam, Valley Spring.

Test your understanding answers

Exercise 1 – Marking exercise

Answer	Marker's comments	Marks
Suitability of online recruitment		
Lots of companies use online recruitment. Online recruitment involves advertising the role online and also possibly gathering applications through an online portal. Large companies will have a very attractive section of the website devoted to recruitment which will have all the roles advertised as well as information about the company and benefits of working with them.	This is a very general introduction and doesn't really add much value. It also focusses too much on large companies, which is not really relevant to MW.	0
MW could use online recruitment to improve the efficiency of the recruitment process and therefore reduce costs. This would be particularly appropriate as there are likely to several new roles to fill when the new factory opens.	This is a valid advantage of online recruitment and also links back to the specific information in the scenario – a good start!	1
This method of recruitment would also be much quicker than any other method.	Although speed of recruitment is mentioned in the marking guide, this point lacks sufficient explanation to earn credit. You need to consider why it is quicker and why this is important for MW.	0

Using online recruitment would allow MW to reach a wider pool of applicants. This may be important as they are trying to recruit a relatively large number of staff from the same area and may not have sufficient word of mouth capabilities to reach enough potential recruits.	Another good point which considers MW.	1
Using online recruitment is more dynamic so the advert and information can be easily amended if the situation changes, for example if a role is filled. This is not the case with other more static methods such as newspaper adverts.	Although this point is not mentioned in the marking guide it is still valid and appropriately explained and so can still earn credit.	1
One problem with online recruitment for MW is they are unlikely to have the relevant IT skills to create the website themselves and so there may be a cost involved.	Another relevant point.	1
Total marks awarded for this element		4

Answer	Marker's comments	Marks
Other methods		
As MW is looking to recruit in the same area it could use its current workforce to help to advertise. They could use job boards in the offices and factory to make staff aware of the vacancies and maybe even offer incentives to staff if they introduce a new successful applicant. This may well be cheaper than other recruitment methods. There is a danger that staff will introduce lots of unsuitable candidates to try and earn the incentive and this could prove costly and take up lots of management time. Staff may also be upset if their introductions are not successful and may resent those who do get the job.	Using word of mouth is a valid suggestion and explained properly. Further detail is given to earn another mark. However this answer goes into too much detail for one point and moves away from the issue slightly by considering all the problems which may arise from offering incentives – which is not even suggested in the scenario. Try not to get too obsessed with one point – you should be aiming for breadth of ideas.	2
MW could use the job centre to assist in recruitment as this will attract a wide number of people. However this may then take time to sort through all of the applications.	This will earn a mark.	1
Other methods include newspaper adverts.	Unfortunately the time spent on the first point has meant there is insufficient time available to complete the answer properly. These points are not explained sufficiently to earn credit.	0
Total marks awarded for this element		3

Answer	Marker's comments	Marks
Impact on financial statements		
The property will initially be recognised at cost in the statement of financial position. Cost includes purchase price and associated professional fees.	This will earn two marks. The point could have been further explained by using the relevant figures given in the scenario.	2
The property will then be depreciated over the useful economic life of the asset. Depreciation will reduce the value of the asset and will also reduce profit each year. The amount depreciated will be reduced by the residual value of the asset (what it is likely to be worth at the end of its life).	Another two marks here but again the use of numbers would be useful.	2
If the property increases in value it can be revalued upwards in future years. This increase in value would be shown in reserves rather than profit.	Although relatively brief this makes the point clearly. An easy mark on subsequent expenditure has been missed and highlights the need to revise the relevant standards thoroughly.	1

If the property suffers a long term reduction in value it will have to be impaired. This involves reducing the value of the property but unlike an upwards revaluation this impairment will reduce profit. This is the principle of prudence.	This also earns a mark. The last sentence is unnecessary.	1
Total marks awarded for this element		6
Total marks awarded	**Fail**	**13**
Total available		25

This answer is significantly shorter than the suggested solutions but is very close to scoring enough to pass. If the advice given above is followed then a comfortable pass would not take much more effort.

Feb. 2015 exam – preseen information

Chapter learning objectives

1 Introduction

In earlier chapters we used the first pilot case (MW) to walk through the processes and approach required for the case study. We now repeat that process using the February 2015 exam (Valley Spring) to give you further insight and experience.

2 Reference Material 1

Background

Valley Spring bottles and sells spring water in Country A. Country A is in Northern Europe and Valley Spring is based in the Northern hilly region of the country. Country A is not at present part of the Eurozone and Country A's currency is the A$.

The region in which Valley Spring is situated is noted for its spring water outlets. Water running down the mountain streams enters the ground on the higher slopes gradually filtering through the rocks and after a number of years re-emerges from a number of springs on the lower slopes.

Valley Spring has its origins as a sheep farm situated on the lower slopes where a number of springs emerge from the ground. This provides a ready source of drinking water for the sheep which continue to thrive in this environment.

25 years ago the owner of the farm, Samuel Taylor, started bottling and selling the water. He had noticed an increasing trend for the sale of bottled spring water as people became more health conscious. At around the same time a number of large well-known soft drinks companies were also exploiting the trend for healthy alternatives to the existing piped water supply. A number of bottled spring waters appeared on the market, and were very successful.

Tests for purity and mineral content of the spring water confirmed that it was safe for human consumption. As a result Mr Taylor investigated the necessary processes required to safely bottle and distribute the water. After some preliminary basic calculations he decided to invest in the bottled water business and production commenced in 1990.

Current position

Valley Spring has grown and has revenue of more than A$ 40 million for the year to 31 December 2014 (the most recent financial statements are included in reference material 2). It bottles and sells both still and sparkling water in two standard sizes of plastic bottle under the brand name Valley Spring. The bottle sizes are 250 ml and 750 ml.

Valley Spring has three customers: two supermarket chains and a major wholesaler who distributes Valley Spring's products to small retailers. All three have several depots at various locations in Country A.

Manufacturing process

The original bottling factory is located next to the spring which was chosen as the most suitable to bottle from. A survey indicated that of the several springs located on the farm land, this one would be the most productive as the water flow was much higher than the others, although over time it was thought possible that other springs may be viable for bottling.

This original plant was expanded eight years ago with the assistance of government grants and there has been no major expansion since then. The original farm business is still in operation but is completely separate from the bottling business.

The manufacturing process is very straightforward at present, the spring is owned by the Taylor family, and the only product costs involved are the bottles, labels for the bottles and the carbon dioxide gas used to produce the sparkling variety by carbonating the water.

Given that the water is for human consumption the majority of the costs result from the bottling process, ensuring that the plant is run to the necessary levels of hygiene and cleanliness. Efficiency and quality control are regarded as of the highest importance.

Distribution

The distribution department operates a fleet of 15 large articulated vehicles and employs 22 staff, a manager, a supervisor and 20 drivers. The department is responsible for delivering to the three customer's depots which are spread geographically over the whole of Country A. The fleet operates for most of the year.

Occasionally the fleet is used to undertake haulage contracts for other organisations, if suitable loads can be found, and the routes are geographically compatible with the delivery journeys. At present this is only done on an occasional basis.

Marketing and product development

The marketing and product development department is the most recent addition to the organisation originally only employing a marketing manager Mr Tom Ford. He is responsible for keeping an overall view on the market and developing trends. As a result of some of his market observations and suggestions, a product development manager Mr John Bond has recently joined the business to investigate further development possibilities.

People involved

The business is still owned by the Taylor family who are the only shareholders.

Samuel Taylor, the founder, is Chairman and Chief Executive. Now aged 60, he has expressed his wish to retire from the business gradually over the next few years.

His son Mark Taylor is currently the Production Director, responsible for production, quality control and distribution. He has already taken over some of his father's duties and has many ideas for the future of the business.

Claire Taylor, Samuel's daughter is the Finance Director, and as such is responsible for the financial and administration functions of the business. She has no formal finance qualification.

The business currently employs 190 staff and is divided into four departments, each with a manager reporting to the appropriate director.

The production department is the largest, employing 155 staff, reporting to Mark Taylor through the production manager, and production supervisors. 10 employees also work exclusively on quality control.

Claire Taylor is responsible for the finance and administration department which currently employs 10 staff including yourself. You have recently been recruited as a finance trainee, assisting in the day to day routines of the department, production of the monthly management reports, year-end financial reports and other reports as required. The manager of the finance team has recently left the business and Claire has assumed these responsibilities until a suitable replacement can be found.

3 Reference Material 2

Statement of Profit or Loss for Valley Spring for the year ended 31 December

	2014 A$000	2013 A$000
Revenue	40,560	39,690
Cost of sales	(22,308)	(22,065)
Gross profit	18,252	17,625
Distribution costs	(12,168)	(11,113)
Administrative expenses	(2,415)	(2,400)
Finance costs	(100)	(135)
Profit before tax	3,569	3,977
Tax	(803)	(908)
Profit for the year	**2,766**	**3,069**

Statement of Financial Position of Valley Spring at 31 December

	2014 A$000	2014 A$000	2013 A$000	2013 A$000
ASSETS				
Non-current assets				
Property, plant and equipment		15,430		16,100
Current assets				
Inventories	2,608		2,540	
Trade and other receivables	8,420		8,102	
Cash and cash equivalents	1,800		1,275	
		12,828		11,917
Total Assets		28,258		28,017

EQUITY AND LIABILITIES

Ordinary share capital issued		500	500
Retained earnings		18,778	17,862
Total equity		19,278	18,362
Non-current liabilities			
Bank loan		1,500	2,250
Current liabilities			
Trade and other payables	6,700		6,490
Tax payable	780		915
		7,480	7,405
Total equity and liabilities		28,258	28,017

Statement of Changes in Equity for Valley Spring for the year ended 31 December 2014

	Share capital A$000	Share premium A$000	Retained earnings A$000	Total A$000
Balance at 1 January 2014	500	–	17,862	18,362
Profit for the year	–	–	2,766	2,766
Dividends paid	–	–	(1,850)	(1,850)
Balance at 31 December 2014	500	–	18,778	19,278

Statement of Cash Flows for Valley Spring for the year ended 31 December 2014

	A$000	A$000
Cash flows from operating activities		
Profit before tax	3,569	
Adjustments		
Depreciation	670	
Finance costs	100	
	4,339	
Movements in working capital		
Increase in inventories	(68)	
Increase in trade and other receivables	(318)	
Increase in trade payables	210	
Cash generated from operations	4,163	
Tax paid	(938)	
Finance costs paid	(100)	
Net cash from operating activities		3,125
Cash flows from financing activities		
Dividend paid	(1,850)	
Loan repayment	(750)	
Net cash from financing activities		(2,600)
Net increase in cash and cash equivalents		525
Cash and cash equivalents at the beginning of the year		1,275
Cash and cash equivalents at the end of the year		1,800

4 Reference Material 3

COSTING REPORT FOR THE YEAR ENDING 31 DECEMBER 2015

Budgeted gross profit statement for the year ending 31 December 2015

	Still 250 ml	Still 750 ml	Sparkling 250 ml	Sparkling 750 ml	Total
Budgeted Sales and production (number of bottles)	5,800,000	9,200,000	5,800,000	12,100,000	
Selling price per bottle (in A$)	0.60	1.40	0.70	1.70	
Budgeted sales revenue (in A$)	3,480,000	12,880,000	4,060,000	20,570,000	40,990,000
Number of batches of production (where a batch is 1,000 bottles)	5,800	9,200	5,800	12,100	
	A$	A$	A$	A$	A$
Sales revenue per batch of 1,000 bottles (A)	600.00	1,400.00	700.00	1,700.00	
Production costs per batch of 1,000 bottles:					
Bottle costs	150.00	250.00	150.00	250.00	
Label costs	15.00	25.00	15.00	25.00	
Gas costs	–	–	35.00	105.00	
Direct production labour costs	33.00	99.00	34.50	103.50	
Total variable prediction costs (B)	198.00	374.00	234.50	483.50	
Contribution per batch of 1,000 bottles (A – B)	402.00	1,026.00	465.50	1,216.50	
Production overhead per batch of 1,000 bottles (C)	137.41	412.24	143.66	430.97	
Gross profit per batch of 1,000 bottles (A – B – C)	264.59	613.76	321.84	785.53	
Total gross profit	1,534,622	5,646,592	1,866,672	9,504,913	18,552,799

Assumptions used in the preparation of the above budgeted gross profit statement:

(1) Inventory levels are not expected to change and therefore production volume and sales volume are equal.

(2) Direct production labour hours are initially measured per 1,000 litres of water and then converted into a cost per batch of 1,000 bottles of product (see working).

(3) All costs other than plastic bottles, labels, gas and direct production labour are treated as fixed costs and are absorbed into production on the basis of direct production labour hours.

Workings

Direct production labour:

Number of direct production labour hours per 1,000 litres of water:

	Still Water Labour hours	Sparkling Water Labour Hours
Extraction	1.30	1.30
Bottling	11.90	12.50
Total labour hours per 1,000 litres	**13.20**	**13.80**

Analysis of direct production hours per batch of 1,000 bottles:

	Still 250 ml	Still 750 ml	Sparkling 250 ml	Sparkling 750 ml
Bottle size as a % of a litre	25%	75%	25%	75%
Therefore number of litres required for a batch of 1,000 bottles (in litres)	250	750	250	750
Number of hours for 1,000 litres (in hours) – taken from table above	13.20	13.20	13.80	13.80
Therefore hours per batch of 1,000 bottles (in hours)	3.30	9.90	3.45	10.35
Rate per hour (in A$)	10	10	10	10
Therefore direct production labour cost per batch of 1,000 bottles (in A$)	**33.00**	**99.00**	**34.50**	**103.50**

Total direct production labour hours:

	Still 250 ml	Still 750 ml	Sparkling 250 ml	Sparkling 750 ml	Total
Number of batches of 1,000 bottles	5,800	9,200	5,800	12,100	
Number of hours per batch of 1,000 bottles (in hours)	3.30	9.90	3.45	10.35	
Therefore total number of hours (in hours)	**19,140**	**91,080**	**20,010**	**125,235**	**255,465**

Production overhead:

Budgeted annual production overhead:

	A$
Energy	6,800,000
Depreciation	670,000
Quality control	215,000
Production management	442,000
Other packaging	560,000
Hire machinery	450,000
Other production costs	1,500,000
Total annual budgeted production overhead	**10,637,000**

Production overhead absorption rate:

Total annual budgeted production overhead (in A$)	10,637,000
Total budgeted direct production labour hours (in hours)	255,465
Therefore, production overhead absorption rate (in A4 per hour)	41.64

Production overhead cost per batch of 1,000 bottles:

	Still 250 ml	Still 750 ml	Sparkling 250 ml	Sparkling 750 ml
Hours per batch of 1,000 bottles (in hours)	3.30	9.90	3.45	10.35
Rate per hour in (A$)	41.64	41.64	41.64	41.64
Therefore production overhead cost per batch of 1,000 bottles (in A$)	**137.41**	**412.24**	**143.66**	**430.97**

5 Reference Material 4

TAX REGIME IN COUNTRY A:

Corporate Profits:

- The corporate tax rate applicable to taxable profits is 30%.

- Unless otherwise stated, accounting rules on recognition and measurement are followed for tax purposes.

- The following expenses are not allowable for tax purposes:
  - accounting depreciation;
  - amortisation;
  - entertaining expenditure;
  - donations to political parties; and
  - taxes paid to other public bodies.

- Tax depreciation allowances are available on items of plant and machinery (including vehicles used for business purposes) at a rate of 25% per year on a reducing balance basis.

- Tax losses can be carried forward to offset against future taxable profits from the same business.

6 Reference Material 5

In the news

Trade journal article about Valley Spring and the Chairman

Spring – a new era approaches:

Valley Spring sits proudly as one of the top three suppliers of bottled water in Country A. Its reputation has been built upon the purity of its water, drawn from its own mountain springs and its belief in a "simple is best" approach.

In a recent interview with Samuel Taylor, founder and current Chairman, he stated that "Valley Spring started out as a bit of an experiment 25 years ago. I originally inherited the family farm 30 years ago but soon realised that with the mountainous nature of the land that I was always going to struggle to make much of a living, especially with the price of sheep at an all-time low back then. So, I looked for alternative ways of using the land and given the number of natural springs it just seemed right to explore the possibility of bottling water and selling it, after all the main ingredient was free."

Samuel Taylor plays down his success and believes that luck had a large part to play. Just as production started, demand for bottled spring water exploded and Samuel believes that ultimately he was in the right place at the right time. Notwithstanding Samuel's humility the Valley Spring brand grew from strength to strength and within 10 years of starting had become one of Country A's major suppliers of bottled water. Valley Spring now accounts for 10% of the market in Country A and in its most recent financial statements posted revenue of over A$ 40 million, equivalent to sales of almost 19 million litres of water.

When asked about the future Samuel Taylor readily admits that the time is fast approaching for him to retire and as a result he has been guiding his children, Mark and Claire to take over the business. In our interview he states "I'm happy for the children to take over now. I feel like I've done my bit. We've maintained market share over the last 10 years by keeping our products simple and pure, but there are so many opportunities out there. I've not got the energy anymore, but they have, so exciting times ahead for the business I'm sure."

He continues. "There are so many ways we can develop and diversify the business, flavoured water is becoming more and more popular and our distribution operation now covers the whole of the country, offering many logistical opportunities. Identifying our brand and bottles as our unique product and expanding into the ever increasing supermarket sector are all possibilities. Now we have a secure base I'm sure the business will grow and succeed."

7 Reference Material 6

The Association of Bottled Water Producers in Country A

INDUSTRY REPORT FOR 2014 AND BEYOND

Introductory message from the Chief Executive

Welcome to this, the 25th annual report of The Association of Bottled Water Producers in Country A. It has been an exciting year with increasing consumption being more than matched with increased production within our own industry. For the first year ever, imports of bottled water by volume have fallen, showing perhaps the growing strength of our industry to compete globally. The effects of the global recession seem firmly behind us this year, which is a trend identified throughout the world.

Looking ahead, there are exciting innovations arising in the industry and the future looks bright!

Fredrick Brown

Chief Executive

Global consumption statistics for 2014:

Global bottled water consumption for 2014 by key market is as follows:

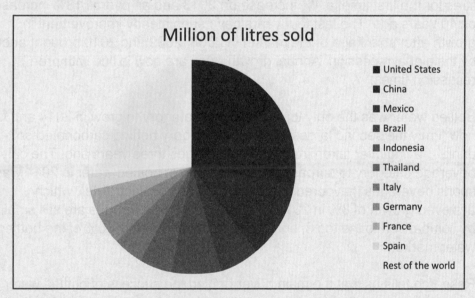

Million of litres sold

- United States
- China
- Mexico
- Brazil
- Indonesia
- Thailand
- Italy
- Germany
- France
- Spain
- Rest of the world

Global bottled water consumption per capita:

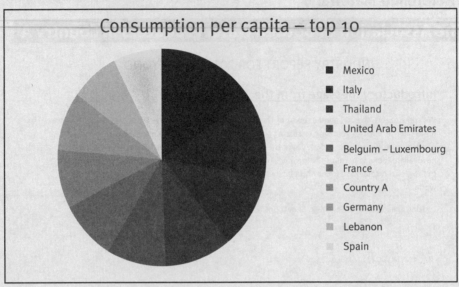

Consumption per capita – top 10

- Mexico
- Italy
- Thailand
- United Arab Emirates
- Belguim – Luxembourg
- France
- Country A
- Germany
- Lebanon
- Spain

Country A ranks 34th in terms of global consumption in absolute terms, but is 7th in terms of consumption per capita.

Analysis of Global Market:

During 2014, global consumption of bottled water grew to over 300 billion litres for the first time, a 4% increase on 2013 and an overall 18% increase on 10 years ago. The last four years have seen steady improvement in growth after shrinkage of the market in 2008, 2009 and 2010 brought about by the global recession. Annual growth rates are now in line with pre-recession times.

Bottled water was the only top 3 beverage category to grow in 2014 and is now firmly the second largest beverage category behind carbonated soft-drinks, having over-taken fruit based beverages three years ago. The only beverage category to surpass the growth rate of bottled water in 2014 was sports beverages (flavoured waters with a dash of electrolyte), which achieved growth of 8% in 2014. However, sports beverages are still small by comparison to the top 3, equivalent to approximately 10% of the bottled water market.

Research tells us that the main driver behind the success of bottled water as a beverage of choice is that the global market is becoming more health conscious. With a potential global obesity crisis looming much has been made by health professionals on the benefits of drinking water, which has undoubtedly helped to boost consumption.

The type of water being bottled varies significantly by country. Globally the split of table and purified water (essentially water sourced from rivers) versus mineral and spring water remains at 60% to 40%, however there are a number of countries where the split is 90%/10% in either direction. Typically European countries prefer mineral and spring water with a number of producers being in existence for over 100 years.

Still water still outstrips sparkling water consumption. Approximately 4 times as much still water is consumed than sparkling, although the gap is slowly falling.

Country A statistics and Analysis:

Volumes consumed, produced, imported and exported

	Consumption (litres billion)	Production (litres billion)	Exported (litres billion)	Imported (litres billion)
2014	2.64	1.79	0.25	1.10
2013	2.51	1.62	0.22	1.11
2012	2.30	1.44	0.18	1.04
2011	2.14	1.30	0.15	0.99

Since 2011, the following annual growth has been achieved:

- 7.3% annual growth in consumption

- 11.3% annual growth in Country A production

- 18.6% annual growth in exports of Country A production

- 3.6% annual growth on imports into Country A

Thus, production of bottled water in Country A is growing at a faster rate than consumption, with this increased production contributing to both increased exports of Country A bottled water and a relative reduction in the reliance on imports. Indeed in 2014 we can see that imports of bottled water by volume have actually fallen for the first time. Country A's bottled water market is strong and indeed growth is outstripping many of our European neighbours.

The proven excellent quality in terms of mineral content and purity of Country A's water is a large part of the reason for both the increase in overall demand within the country and the increase in exports.

Break-down of Country A consumption by type of bottled water:

Type of bottled water

- Mineral
- Spring
- Table
- Purified

Mineral and spring water together account for 84% of Country A's consumption, with purified and table waters together only contributing 16%. This statistic remains largely unchanged for the last five years and is a clear indication of consumer preference.

There has, however, been a slight change in the preference between still and sparkling water. Still water now accounts for 70% of total bottled water consumption, against 30% for sparkling water. Five years ago still water was 60% against 40% for sparkling.

Interestingly, however, there are a couple of new trends emerging – flavoured waters and isotonic enhanced water (see next section).

The future for Country A's bottled water producers:

The future appears to be promising. We anticipate that global demand for bottled water of all types will continue to expand. Within this general expansion we expect a significant increase in the demand for natural mineral and spring waters resulting from the continued prevalence of opinions from health professionals that such waters have natural health benefits. Country A already has a reputation for good quality mineral and spring water and therefore Country A's producers are well placed to take advantage of this global trend.

There are also some interesting developments in the types of water sold. Natural water flavoured with fruit syrups are starting to emerge with many producers starting to experiment with flavour combinations and packaging options to boost consumption. Isotonic enhanced mineral water is also new into the market and could potentially be huge as consumers become ever more sports and health conscious.

8 Summary

We are now working through the February 2015 exam from beginning to end so you can see all of the skills and techniques which may be required in this exam. This chapter simply reproduces the pre-seen information and we will work through this in more detail in the next two chapters.

Next steps:

(1) Make sure you have at least skim read the pre-seen before moving on.

(2) It might be useful to make a list at this point of what you think some of the relevant technical areas might be – are you comfortable with these areas?

Feb. 2015 exam – summary of the pre-seen

Chapter learning objectives

- To apply the techniques covered in chapter 5 to the February 2015 real exam pre-seen.

1 Introduction

In the chapter 5 we showed you some techniques to help you in your analysis of the pre-seen.

Once you have completed your analysis of the pre-seen for the February 2015 paper you can review this chapter to ensure you have identified the key points. We will take you through each exhibit highlighting the key conclusions before bringing this together into a summary using the SWOT framework.

2 Exhibit by exhibit analysis

The key issues and conclusions that could have been brought out of the pre-seen exhibits are as follows:

Reference material 1: Introduction

(Note: in the pilot there were plenty of clues in ex1 as to possible end-games and requirements)

Background

- VS sells mineral water in Country A
- Competition from well known soft drinks companies

Current position

- Only three customers, all of whom are major – is there a threat from high customer power? (E1)

Manufacturing process

- Water taken from one spring – opportunity of opening more to boost supply.
- Is there a risk it could dry up or get contaminated?
- If the spring got blocked, thus reducing supply, then VS might have to decide whether to prioritise selling still or sparkling (P1)
- Previous expansion involved government grants (F1)
- Original farm business still operating – could there be cross-contamination – e.g. via the use of farm chemicals?
- "Efficiency and quality control are regarded as of the highest importance." – expect problems in one of the exam variants.

Distribution

- Have to cover the whole of the country. VS only do a small amount of haulage for third parties, so presumably most deliveries result in empty lorries returning to the bottling plant. They may wish to try to improve efficiency.

Marketing and product development

- This is a new department, so expect new proposals/initiatives in the exam.

People

- Samuel Taylor currently Chairman **and** CEO – governance best practice would suggest that these two roles should be separated

- Mark Taylor – "new ideas"

- Claire Taylor is not a qualified finance professional but has taken over the finance department after the previous manager left. This definitely sets us up to have to advise her/explain to her accounting treatments (F1) and possibly budgeting/costing issues (P1)

- Functional structure fine for now with such a limited product range but growth/expansion could lead us into considering whether to switch to divisional (E1)

Reference material 2 – Financial statements

Comments

- Encouraging to see revenue growth of 2.2% (W), although this could simply be due to inflation (i.e. *real* growth minimal). Note: When we get to ex6 we realise that VS's growth is disappointing compared to overall country stats.

- Slight increase in gross margins from 44.4% to 45.0% also encouraging – could be due to higher prices (reflecting brand strength) or to good cost control. Don't have sufficient information to explore further at this stage.

- However, distribution costs have risen as a % of sales from 28% to 30% (nice round numbers suggest this is very intentional from the writer's perspective), resulting in a fall in profit before (and after) tax. We are not told why distribution costs have gone up.

- Also level of PPE has fallen, suggesting a lack of investment, maybe because Samuel is retiring and has starting stepping back from decision making?

- Short operating cycle indicating that working capital shouldn't be a big problem unless they make it one due to inefficiencies, etc.

- From the statement of CF we can see that working capital has grown by a net A$176k, so might be worth watching out for.

- Bank loan and gearing reduced. This is good but off syllabus at this level!

- Large dividend paid (1,850 is 67% of the profit after tax figure of 2,766) – is this sustainable, especially if looking to develop new products and expand?

- High levels of cash – scenario could look at investing in growth or ask you to discuss possible short term investments (e.g. CDs, etc) plus criteria

Workings

Ratio	2014	2013
Revenue growth	2.2%	–
Gross profit margin	45.0%	44.4%
Distribution costs as a % of sales	30.0%	28.0%
Receivables days	76	75
Payables days (Note)	110	107
Inventory days	43	42
Length of operating cycle	9	10

Note: have used cost of sales to calculate payables days – would ideally use purchases but don't have the information.

Reference material 3 – Costing Statements

Context

- Have 4 products – still v sparkling, 250 v 750ml

- Valley Spring do monthly management reports (ex1) and budgeting exercises (ex3 here)

- Note: Be careful when using these statements – especially whether using litres or bottles.

Comments on statement

- Budgeted revenue = A\$ 40,990k, an increase of 1.06% which is very conservative, indicating the need for new ideas to achieve growth.

- Sparkling water commands higher prices than still

- Looking at sales revenue, the budgeted mix split is 39.9% still to 60.1% sparkling. Production plans do not reflect country demand – VS sells more sparkling than still but in the country as a whole the demand is 70:30 (ex6) in favour of still.

- Contribution margins suggest that larger bottles are better than smaller and still water is better than sparkling

- Gross profit margins change this assessment – now sparkling is better than still but the differences between smaller and larger bottles is more marginal

- Do we consider changing the mix? At operational level it is more likely that someone else will suggest changing the mix and we explain the basis of calculations or look at implications, reservations, implementation aspects.

- Sparkling water uses more bottling labour so gets apportioned proportionately more OH.

- Are labour hours the best basis for absorption?

- Energy costs are very significant – is there scope to reduce these? Could we be criticised for a poor record on sustainability?

- Suppose there was a labour shortage, key factor analysis would suggest prioritising the products in the order 250ml sparkling > 250ml still > 750ml sparkling > 750ml still.

Calculations

	Still 250 ml	Still 750 ml	Sparkling 250 ml	Sparkling 750 ml
Contribution margin	67.0%	73.3%	66.5%	71.6%
Gross profit margin	44.1%	43.8%	46.0%	46.2%
Contribution/labour hour (calcs done for batch of 1,000 bottles)	402.00/3.30 = 121.82	1,026.00/9.90 = 103.64	465.50/3.45 = 134.93	1,216.50/10.35 = 117.54

Reference material 4 – Tax regime

- Tax is covered in F1, so you might have to explain some tax issues to Claire – for example, to review a tax calc prepared by Claire that contains errors (e.g. not separating out disallowable expenses)?

Reference material 5 – Article

- VS is a top 3 supplier in Country A with 10% market share (p12)
- Samuel talks about "maintaining" market share, again suggesting he perhaps lacked ambition (and energy) in recent years to grow the business
- Opportunities identified:
  - flavoured water.
  - logistical opportunities – presumably offering haulage to 3rd parties?
  - expanding into the ever increasing supermarket sector – possibly own brands

Reference material 6 – Industry Report

This exhibit gives useful information for identifying potential opportunities and threats.

- Firms in Country A competing well against imports suggesting an export policy may be successful for some?
- Country A ranks high in terms of consumption per head suggesting a saturated market and the need to look elsewhere for growth?
- 4% growth in global demand for bottled water but 8% for sports beverages – might be an opportunity for VS?
- Country A statistics indicate that VS growth disappointing:
  - 7.3% growth in consumption
  - 11.3% growth in production
- Other firms in Country A are growing via the export market – why not VS?
- Other trends
  - Switch to still instead of sparkling (70:30 compared with 60:40 five years ago)
  - Global opportunities due to health benefits of spring water
  - Growth in demand for flavoured waters and isotonic drinks for sports

3 SWOT analysis

As discussed in chapter 6, a SWOT analysis is a useful tool to summarise the current position of the company. A SWOT analysis can be presented simply as a list of strengths, followed by weaknesses, then opportunities and finally threats. It would be useful to indicate within each category which factors seem more significant than others, perhaps by listing them in descending order of priority.

Test Your Understanding

Prepare a SWOT analysis of Valley Spring based on the summary of each exhibit.

Strengths	Weaknesses
Opportunities	**Threats**

4 Summary

You should now be comfortable with all the key issues identified in the VS pre-seen and ready to start thinking about the exam.

Next steps:

(1) It is a good idea, once you have analysed the pre-seen, to brainstorm a list of possible triggers (what might happen) and tasks (what you have to do) which you may face in the exam.

This is NOT an exercise in question spotting as you cannot hope to simply guess the requirements and only study a limited amount of topics.

However this brainstorm will help you to think about how the pre-seen may relate to the competencies and may mean fewer complete surprises on the day of the exam.

Test your understanding answers

Strengths	Weaknesses
• Top 3 supplier in Country A with 10% market share	• Increase in distribution costs
• Financially strong – low gearing, good cash flow	• Claire Taylor is not a qualified finance professional but has taken over the finance department after the previous manager left
• 10 employees focus on quality control	• Limited product portfolio
• Own fleet of distribution vehicle	• Could suggest that Samuel has lacked ambition – lack of investment in PPE for example
	• Haven't really matched production to market trends – e.g. mix of still v sparkling
	• Reliance on three large customers

Opportunities	Threats
• New products – flavoured water, isotonic enhanced water	• Contamination of water from various means
• New markets – exports	• Competition from large soft drinks companies
• New distribution system to save costs	• Only three customers – they may threaten to go to rivals if prices are not dropped
• Open up other springs to boost supply	• Downturn in consumer demand
• Increase business offering haulage to third parties	
• Change mix towards still rather than sparkling	
• Other uses for farmland	

Feb. 2015 exam – variant 1 – unseen information

Chapter learning objectives

1 Introduction

In the Operational level case study variant 1 exam for February 2015 the first screen you were presented with showed the number of requirements and the designated time allocations:

This examination is structured as follows:

Section	Number of tasks	Timing of section
1	1	60 minutes
2	1	50 minutes
3	1	25 minutes
4	1	45 minutes

The time available in each section is for reading, planning and writing your response(s).

This information will be available for you to access during the examination by clicking on the pre-seen button.

2 Unseen information – requirements

The exam then continues and you are presented with the following screens.

SECTION 1

Section 1 – Screen 1 – trigger

Today is 2 March 2015. and as you arrive at work you read the following notice which has been put on on the internal staff notice board by Mark Taylor, Valley Spring's Production Director.

Flavoured Water – the way forward!

I'm thrilled to announce that we will soon be embarking on an exciting expansion plan here at Valley Spring. Thanks to the work undertaken by John Bond, our new product development manager, it has been decided by the directors to broaden our product base by starting to produce and sell flavoured water and I already have indications from our customers that they will be placing orders once available.

So, lots to look forward to and exciting times ahead. There will obviously be some disruption as we work out the new production plans. If the launch is successful we will install a new production line in the longer term.

After market research our plan is to launch 2 flavours (cherry and raspberry) in our standard 750 ml bottles in both our still and sparkling varieties. All being well we hope to launch other flavours at a later date.

Section 1 – Screen 2 – task

Today is 16 March 2015 and you receive the following email from Claire Taylor:

From: Claire Taylor, ct@vspring.com
Sent: 16th March 2015, 1.30 p.m.
Subject: Flavoured water production

At the management meeting yesterday it was decided that with minimal alteration to the existing production line we should be able to start production of the flavoured water from 1 April 2015. We already have tentative orders from our customers for the flavoured water, however, I'm not convinced in the short term we actually have enough capacity to meet these orders. I'm reluctant to take on more employees at this stage because we don't know how well the flavoured water will sell.

A good friend of mine, who is an accountant, pulled together some numbers for me last night based on our budgeted standard costs and expected production of all products for the next 3 months. She has established that if we set our production to meet all of our orders, then we will need 80,630 direct production hours, although (on the assumption that we do not take on any more staff), we only have 72,000 hours available, a shortfall of 8,680.

She has prepared her analysis on the basis of a batch of 1,000 bottles for each of our six products, which are:

- the four existing products, as included in our costing report, plus

- 750 ml bottle of flavoured still water; and

- 750 ml bottle of flavoured sparkling water.

Clearly we need to decide which of our six products to focus on. Personally, I would have thought that we should focus on those products with the highest gross profit per batch of 1,000 bottles. As a result my suggestion would be to focus production on the larger bottles. I see my friend has calculated contribution per direct production labour hour, which seems to present a slightly different solution to the problem, so I'm a little confused.

She also mentioned that we should consider whether throughput accounting might be beneficial to us. This means nothing to me at the moment.

Please could you look at the schedule for me which I've attached and explain:

(1) Whether it is appropriate to justify the production decision on the basis of gross profit or contribution per direct production labour hour per batch of 1,000 bottles as shown in the schedule.

(2) Whether there are any other factors we should take into account before setting the production plan for the next three months, including removing the constraint.

(3) What throughput accounting is and whether it might be beneficial to considering using it in our business

Claire Taylor

Finance Director

Valley Spring

Email: ct@vspring.com

Section 1 – reference material

Direct production labour hours required to meet all orders:

The direct production labour hours required to produce all orders for 3 months from 1 April 2015 are calculated in the following table:

	Still	Still	Sparkling	Sparkling	Still flavoured	Still flavoured
	250 ml	750 ml	250 ml	750 ml	750ml	750ml
Number of batches required	1,450	2,300	1,450	3,025	750	750
Direct production labour hours required	4,785	22.770	5,003	31,309	8,213	8,550

Total hours required to meet all our anticipated orders is 80,630 hours. Maximum available is 72,000 hours.

Schedule of budgeted contribution and gross profit by product per batch of 1,000 bottles

Based on the original budget data for the year ended 31 December 2015 and budgets for the new flavoured waters.

Per 1,000 bottles of product.	Still	Still	Sparkling	Sparkling	Still flavoured	Still flavoured
	250 ml	750 ml	250 ml	750 ml	750ml	750ml
	A$	A$	A$	A$	A$	A$
Sales revenue	600	1,400	700	1,700	1,600	1,900
Bottle costs	150	250	150	250	280	280
Cost of labels	15	25	15	25	25	25
Cost of gas	–	–	35	105	–	105
Cost of flavouring	–	–	–	–	75	75
Direct production labour	33	99	35	105	110	114
Contribution	**402**	**1,026**	**465**	**1,215**	**1,110**	**1,301**
Production overhead *	137	412	144	431	456	475
Gross profit	**265**	**614**	**321**	**784**	**654**	**826**

*Based on the original overhead absorption rate of A$41.64 per direct labour hour.

The direct production labour hours per batch of 1,000 bottles and therefore contribution per direct production labour hour are:

	Still	Still	Sparkling	Sparkling	Still flavoured	Still flavoured
	250 ml	750 ml	250 ml	750 ml	750ml	750ml
Direct production labour hours per batch of 1,000 bottles (hrs)	1,450	2,300	1,450	3,025	750	750
Contribution per hour (A$)	4,785	22.770	5,003	31,309	8,213	8,550

Section 1 – Requirement

Write your response to Claire Taylor in the email below:

To: Claire Taylor, ct@vspring.com
Sent: 16th March 2015
Subject: Flavoured water production

Note: do not attempt this requirement at this stage – you will do this in the next chapter.

SECTION 2

Section 2 – Screen 1 – combined trigger and task

Today is 24 April 2015. The interest in flavoured water has been even greater than expected. Management have decided to construct a new production line within the existing factory space in order to increase capacity. You receive the following email from Claire Taylor:

From: Claire Taylor, ct@vspring.com
Sent: 24th April 2015, 1.30 p.m.
Subject: New production line

Marketing campaign

Production of the new flavoured water is going well so far. We could already sell more than we can produce at the moment but, if we are going to utilise the new line to its maximum, then we do need to grow the market perception of our flavoured brand.

I'm meeting with a marketing agency tomorrow in order to start considering a marketing campaign. It's the first time that I've been involved with this agency and it's the company's first campaign in five years. I'm keen that I don't embarrass myself tomorrow and I know that you've been studying about marketing in your latest examinations. They have asked me to think about the market segments that we want to target. It's important that we get the maximum returns possible from this campaign.

Please let me have an explanation of how market segmentation can help us run the campaign effectively.

Marketing costs and brand value in the financial statements

I'm anticipating that, if we get the campaign right, that we'll be able to greatly enhance the strength of our brand, for both the new flavoured and our existing water products. this in turn should enable us to expand even further in the future and potentially open a new factory. However, in order to do this we would need to secure debt finance from the bank and I know that they will look at our financial statements in order to make their lending decision.

Ideally we need to boost the value of our assets in the statement of financial position as this would make the business look healthier. I've read somewhere that you can capitalise the cost of marketing campaigns and also the value of a brand as intellectual property.

Please let me know with appropriate justification whether this is actually the case.

Many thanks

Claire Taylor
Finance Director
Valley Spring
Email: ct@vspring.com

Section 2 – Requirement

Write your response to Claire Taylor in the box below:

To: Claire Taylor, ct@vspring.com
Sent: 24th April 2015
Subject: Marketing campaign and marketing costs

Note: do not attempt this requirement at this stage – you will do this in the next chapter.

SECTION 3

Section 3 – Screen 1 – combined trigger and task

Today is 15 June 2015 and you are called to Claire Taylor's office where she says the following:

"I've just spoken to the marketing agency, they've been working really hard and our first television adverts will start by the end of the month. All being well, the new production line will also be ready by then so we can start building up our inventory in anticipation of an increase in orders. We have already started recruiting extra staff to start on the 1 July.

Anyway, the reason I wanted to talk to you was that given the new production line and our potential growth, I think it is time we looked at our product costing system. As you know in the past we've always assumed that all direct production labour cost is variable and that all production overhead is fixed.

I would like us to get a better idea of how much of our cost is actually variable and how much is fixed, as we might then be better placed to control them.

Please could you prepare a schedule for me which considers our direct production labour **and** energy costs in terms of:

(1) the likelihood that the costs will be largely fixed or variable in nature, and

(2) how we might better forecast the split between the fixed and variable elements."

Section 3 – Requirement

Write your response to Claire Taylor's request in the box below:

Note: do not attempt this requirement at this stage – you will do this in the next chapter.

SECTION 4

Section 4 – Screen 1 – combined trigger and task

Today is 8 September 2015 and you receive the following email from Claire Taylor:

From: Claire Taylor, ct@vspring.com
Sent: 8th September 2015, 9.45 a.m.
Subject: New customers

The marketing campaign seems to be a big success. Already this morning I've had two more requests from small retailers who don't currently stock our water to sell our products directly to them. So far I've directed them to our wholesale customer but I'm starting to think that maybe we should consider selling directly to small retailers. We've only ever had three customers which works well because they are large entities and pay regularly (even though they demand 60 days credit terms). Please could prepare a brief report that I can use at our next management meeting on the implications of taking on direct selling to small scale customers.

In particular can you please comment on the following:

- the practical impact on the finance function of supplying directly to small scale customers;

- the impact on the risks faced by Valley Spring of supplying directly to small scale customers; and

- any measures that Valley Spring could adopt to manage and mitigate any additional risks.

Many thanks

Claire Taylor
Finance Director
Valley Spring
Email: ct@vspring.com

Section 4 – Requirement

Write the report requested by Claire Taylor in the box below:

Note: do not attempt this requirement at this stage – you will do this in the next chapter.

3 Summary

This chapter has introduced you to the unseen information for the February 2015 variant 1 exam.

Next steps:

(1) You should work through this exam using the unseen information and the following chapter which contains additional guidance to help you with your first attempt. The examiners consider it crucial that any practice you do, such as looking at past exams, is treated like an exam. You should therefore be writing out your own answers before reviewing the suggested solutions. Merely reading the requirements and then the suggested solutions has limited value.

Feb. 2015 exam – variant 1 – walkthrough

Chapter learning objectives

- To gain further experience and develop exam technique by walking through and attempting another case study exam.

1 Exam section 1

Summary of trigger 1

Two new products are being launched and will initially be made using existing facilities and workers, rather than expanding production at this stage. There are insufficient labour hours to meet initial production plans so a decision needs to be made how best to allocate scarce resources. This draws primarily on underlying P1 knowledge.

Stop and think!

(1) You won't need to do any calculations as they have already been done.

(2) Which aspects of P1 relate to decision making with constraints?

(3) Start thinking about the relevant information in the pre-seen. It's very important that your responses are applied to the scenario.

Overview of task 1

You need to prepare an email that covers:

(1) Whether it is appropriate to justify the production decision on the basis of gross profit or contribution per direct production labour hour.

(2) Whether there are any other factors Valley Spring should take into account before setting the production plan for the next three months, including removing the constraint.

(3) What throughput accounting is and whether it might be beneficial to Valley Spring.

Let's plan

We need to create a planning page that ensures you identify and respond to all parts of the requirement. You can use the techniques discussed in Chapter eight or develop your own method. Here we will use the ordered list approach, focussing on key questions you should be asking yourself.

Split your planning sheet (use your wipe clean whiteboard) into a grid to ensure all three parts are covered. Your thought process could go as follows:

Production decision

- What decision making techniques can you remember from P1?

- Which ones deal with decision making with constraints – direct production labour is limited here?

- How do the two approaches suggested in the email correlate to your P1 knowledge?

- As well as this more theoretical P1 emphasis, are there simple practical issues to incorporate, such as problems determining the figures in the first place?

- Given the above, what are the pros and cons of using gross profit?

- Similarly, what are the pros and cons of using contribution per direct production labour hour

Other factors

- Start by considering how the constraint could be removed - note that the task states "including..." – can more hours be made available? How? What are the potential problems with this?

- What other factors are relevant – try to consider non-financial aspects as the discussion so far has concentrated on financial issues.

Throughput accounting

- To start you simply need to explain what throughput accounting is. Ideally your explanation will refer to Valley Spring to illustrate points.

- The second aspect is more tricky here – what are the advantages and disadvantages of throughput accounting and how do they relate to Valley Spring – application is key here.

Finally you may wish to consider how best to split the 60 minutes for task 1 between the different elements, to ensure that you address all sub-requirements.

As a rough rule of thumb you should spend about 15–20% of the time available for reading and planning. So for this section of the exam, where you are given 60 minutes, you should be spending approximately 10 minutes planning your answer before you complete the exercise below. This would leave you about 50 minutes to write your answer and a few minutes spare to check through what you have written.

Exercise 1

Prepare a response to the first task in the February 2015 – variant 1 – exam.

2 Exam section 2

Summary of trigger 2

Valley Spring is now considering expansion to meet increasing demand and is planning to build a new production line. Task 2 looks at the expansion in terms of the impact on marketing (E1) and the possibility of strengthening the statement of financial position by capitaling marketing costs and valuing the brand (F1).

Stop and think!

(1) Think about your own experiences of marketing to generate some ideas.

(2) Can you remember how segmentation works from your E1 studies?

(3) Can you remember the financial reporting rules for capitalising an asset?

Summary of task 2

Respond to the email as follows:

*   An explanation of how market segmentation can help Valley Spring run the new marketing campaign effectively

*   Whether Valley Spring can capitalise the cost of marketing campaigns and also the value of a brand as intellectual property, with appropriate justification.

Let's plan

You can use the method of planning shown above or refer to Chapter 8 and use a mind map instead. The important thing is to generate some ideas and get the main points in some order before you start to write.

When you are discussing market segmentation think about how it might work at Valley Spring rather than simply listing ways the market could be segmented. Start by thinking about different ways Valley Spring could segment and then, for each, discuss how useful this might be. There are 50 minutes in total for task 2, so you really need to address a range of specific methods rather than keeping your answer more generic.

For the second aspect it is vital that you can remember the basic ideas of IAS 38 Intangible Assets, so you can discuss whether or not marketing costs and brand name satisfy the various requirements for recognising assets.

Now spend 8 minutes completing your plan before attempting Exercise 2. You would then have 42 minutes to write your answer and a few minutes to check through what you have written before reviewing the solution.

Exercise 2

Prepare a response to the second task in the February 2015 – variant 1 – exam.

3 Exam section 3

Summary of trigger 3

The case now focusses more specifically on the new production line and whether or not costs are fixed or variable (P1).

Stop and think!

- This is the shortest task at 25 minute, so make you answer the question set as quickly and efficiently as possible otherwise you may run out of time.

- The distinction between fixed and variable costs is a simple concept, so to produce a good answer, it is vital that you discuss how the issues apply to Valley Spring.

Summary of task 3

Prepare a schedule that considers direct production labour **and** energy costs in terms of:

(1) The likelihood that the costs will be largely fixed or variable in nature, and

(2) How Valley Spring might better forecast the split between the fixed and variable elements.

Let's plan

You can use either method of planning here as long as you address all parts of the requirement. Make sure you note what is required carefully – for example you are asked to look at the likelihood that costs will be fixed or variable. This implies that it is not a simple yes/no answer but you need to discuss to what extent costs are fixed/variable. To make this easier you could think about what components make up each cost. You will need such a breakdown when discussing forecasting.

Give yourself about 5 minutes to plan and then you can attempt exercise 3. You will then have about 20 minutes to write your answer, leaving a short amount of time to check through what you have written.

Exercise 3

Prepare a response to the third task in the February 2015 – variant 1 – exam.

4 Exam section 4

Summary of trigger 4

Task 4 looks at expanding the customer base by selling direct to small customers and some of the implications of this, focussing on the finance function (E1) and the subsequent risks and their treatment (E1, P1 and F1!)

Stop and think!

- Currently Valley Spring only has three customers – What difference does this make compared to having many customers?

- To help identify risks, think what could go wrong if we had more customers?

- Alternatively, are there any ways in which having more customers could reduce risks?

- How do companies you are familiar with manage such risks?

Summary of task 4

Write a report addressing the following:

- The practical impact of selling direct to smaller customers on the finance function

- The impact of supplying directly to small scale customers on the risks faced by Valley Spring

- Any measures that Valley Spring could adopt to manage and mitigate any additional risk.

Let's plan

The question asks for a report so start by writing a short introduction – this effectively repeats the requirement.

There are a number of ways of identifying relevant issues for the impact on the finance function:

- You could think about all the different operations that are carried out by the finance function and see which would be affected and how.

- Alternatively you could consider the lifecycle of a customer, starting with what would be involved setting up a new customer and what ongoing interactions would occur.

- Common sense and experience – for example, what difference does it make that the customers are **smaller**?

Whichever approach is adopted, make sure you discuss the practical **impact** on the finance function.

When discussing risks for the second and third elements, the easiest way to identify risks is simply to ask yourself what might go wrong and what they could do to manage such risks. Again the key here is to relate all points to Valley Spring and be as detailed and specific as possible.

Exercise 4

Prepare a response to the final task in the February 2015 – variant 1 – exam.

5 Summary

You should now have a better understanding of how to approach the exam requirements and plan your answer. Although this chapter uses the pilot exam as an example, the techniques used can be applied to any set of exam tasks.

Next steps:

(1) As previously mentioned, you should attempt a written answer yourself to all of the tasks before reviewing the suggested solutions.

(2) Reviewing the solutions may highlight knowledge gaps which you may need to revisit.

Test your understanding answers

Exercise 1

> *These answers have been provided by CIMA for information purposes only. The answers created are indicative of a response that could be given by a good candidate. They are not to be considered exhaustive, and other appropriate relevant responses would receive credit.*
>
> *CIMA will not accept challenges to these answers on the basis of academic judgement.*

Section 1:

To: Claire Taylor, ct@vspring.com
Sent: 16 March 2015
Subject: RE: Flavoured water production

I've looked at the schedule that you sent through and will address each of your queries in turn.

Appropriateness of using gross profit or contribution per direct production labour hour as the basis of the production decision

The gross profit per batch shown in the schedule includes a share of all production costs and therefore can be said to reflect the profit per batch after all production costs have been taken into account. However, there are three main issues with using this measure as currently calculated as a basis upon which to decide the production schedule in this situation.

Firstly, gross profit per batch includes costs which are mostly fixed in nature and therefore have to be incurred irrespective of which products are produced.

Secondly, looking at gross profit per batch in absolute terms does not take into account the fact that we are dealing with a constrained resource here. Whilst, the smaller bottles might generate the lowest levels of gross profit in absolute terms what is more important is how much they generate in terms of an hour of direct production labour as this is our scarce resource.

Finally, the production overheads that have been absorbed into the cost of each batch are based upon the budgeted production overhead absorption rate of A$ 41.64 per direct production labour hour. Given that we are launching two new products it's likely that this rate will increase because firstly, there could be additional overhead cost to incur and secondly, the number of production hours will also increase.

Therefore in this situation where we have a constrained resource it is not appropriate to base our decision on gross profit per batch.

Using contribution per direct labour hour however is more appropriate in this situation because:

It deals with many of the issues about the use of gross profit per batch discussed above, in particular:

Because it's a contribution measure it by definition focuses on those production costs which change as the level of production changes. Ultimately contribution is so called because it's what "contributes" towards fixed costs and profit. Having said that though there is an argument here that the contribution figure used in the schedule is not a true contribution figure because it includes labour costs which might be considered to be fixed in nature due in the short term, especially if the employees are on contracted hours.

It is important when considering a production decision where there is a constraint, that the amount of contribution per unit of that constrained resource is calculated. This is because we need to ensure that we get the maximum benefit from using that resource, by prioritising those products which generate the greatest amount of contribution for each unit of that constrained resource. In our situation our constrained resource is the amount of direct production labour hours available, hence why contribution per direct production labour hour has been calculated.

If we take as an example Sparkling 250ml, this generates the second to lowest level of contribution per batch in absolute terms but actually generates the best contribution per direct production labour hour. This is because it uses only 3.45 hours to produce each batch, whilst the larger bottles take considerably longer.

Other factors to be considered, including removing the constraint:

The results show that to maximise contribution per direct production labour hour that we should not be producing one of our new products (this is because Still flavoured 750 ml has the lowest contribution per direct labour hour). This would potentially be counter-productive as the whole point of expanding production is to launch the products to see how well they sell. Therefore in reality we will need to continue to produce Still flavoured 750 ml and hence Still 750ml production should be curtailed instead.

We also need to consider whether production labour hours are truly constrained. It is possible with some training that we could increase the speed at which staff work, therefore enhancing production. Alternatively we could look into how production is scheduled on the production line to see if it is possible to improve our output from the resources available. I'm sure that Mark would be able to advise on the possibility of this relatively easily.

Another factor to consider is whether the measurement of the hours to produce a batch is accurate. The budget currently calculates hours based on the volume of water alone and ignores the time taken to handle 1,000 bottles on the production line (which is likely to be very similar for each size of bottle).

Finally, we need to consider what sales orders we already have as we will need to honour these orders and ensure that our customers are kept happy.

Throughput accounting:

Throughput accounting is very similar to marginal costing in that it focuses on a contribution measure rather than a total production cost measure as is the case in absorption costing. The basic idea of throughout accounting though is that management should focus on maximising throughput contribution (which is sales revenue less direct material costs) whilst reducing inventory and operational expenses (which are in effect deemed to be fixed in nature), as this will ultimately lead to the greatest efficiency and profit.

In throughput accounting management focus on identifying bottleneck resources (such as direct production labour) and ensuring that such resources are used to 100% of their capacity in a way that maximises throughput contribution. If there are no bottleneck resources then production should be scheduled so as to exactly meet customer demand and no more, otherwise inventory builds up which is inefficient. Where there are bottleneck resources production should be scheduled so that priority is given to products that earn the highest throughput per unit of the bottleneck resource.

The main aim of throughput accounting is that management focus on identifying bottleneck resources within the business with a view to eliminating them as a bottleneck so that customer demand can be met in full. In our case this would mean taking on additional staff or paying overtime to existing staff to increase production hours.

Usefulness to Valley Spring:

Throughput accounting is really a management philosophy rather than a formal cost accounting system despite being called "throughput accounting". Therefore it is not the case that it would replace our existing costing systems per se but that we might be able to apply some of the principles in certain situations.

As mention above throughput accounting focuses on the idea of identifying bottleneck resources and then scheduling production to maximise the throughput contribution. This approach is particularly useful to businesses which have complex manufacturing processes where individual machines or types of skilled labour can be short in supply. Clearly Valley Spring is not such a business because our production process is simple and we only have one type of production labour. Also we only have one bottleneck resource, which is our direct production labour. Therefore throughput accounting as such is likely to be of limited use to us going forward.

In addition, generally speaking, throughput accounting is less useful for making decisions about longer term production planning because ultimately we will be able to take on more staff and assuming that demand for the new products is strong then we might well consider investing in upgrading the existing production line or even installing an additional line.

Exercise 2

To: Claire Taylor, ct@vspring.com
Sent: 24 April 2015
Subject: Marketing campaign and marketing costs

Market segmentation

Market segmentation is the subdividing of the market into homogenous groups to whom a separate marketing mix can be focussed. Put very simply in our case this could be which groups of people buy our bottled water in terms of – how often, which bottles are most popular, how old they are and where they live. So a market segment is a group of consumers with distinct shared needs.

By segmenting the market as described it allows us to treat similar customers in similar ways when marketing our products. Each market segment may have slightly different needs which can be satisfied by offering each one a slightly different marketing mix.

The key to all this is to be able to say that people falling into a particular segment are more likely to purchase the product so that this information can be focussed into the marketing campaign to hopefully gain maximum return. We need to choose a particular segment or segments to target to ensure a cost effective campaign.

For example demographic segmentation may depend on age some flavours more popular with younger consumers, traditional still water with older consumers, likewise with gender. Geographical area may be a factor warmer and urban areas having higher consumption rates. Family life cycle is also a factor young families for example having higher consumption rates of all varieties.

Socio-economic segmentation by occupation and income is also important. People may buy bottled water for convenience, those with higher incomes may purchase higher volumes and more branded varieties.

Psychological aspects are likely to involve lifestyle attitudes, some consumers may prefer bottled spring water to the public supply, and consider this the healthier option.

Situational use such as restaurants and dinner parties, during work time in the office and sporting events all give rise to the opportunity of marketing to particular segments of the market.

In order to do this, these market segments need to be measurable, that is, it must be possible to identify the number of buyers in each segment. For example the number of people aged between 30 and 40 or married with children, which can be found from survey information.

It follows that if in a particular area, for example a heavily populated urban area, people favour flavoured water which is most popular with the 18 to 25 age group, suitable advertising and media can be chosen. More rural areas may show different patterns of consumption for which a different marketing strategy may be appropriate.

Further it is important that these segments are accessible. In our case this is certainly possible. People are not bound to buy our bottled water but neither are they tied to any particular brand. This is an important key feature to be considered as an effective marketing campaign can swing choice in our favour.

Segments should also be substantial. The cost of targeting a particular segment must be less than the benefit and small market segments may prove unprofitable. It is far more likely a city based campaign targeted at a specific age range will yield positive results.

It is important that we consider all of these factors when considering our marketing campaign.

For example demographically some brands of breakfast cereal are popular with young children and are promoted accordingly, daytime early evening TV adverts, those promoting weight loss and health benefits may be shown later in the evening when a more adult audience is anticipated.

Own label products may be popular in lower income areas. In our case our sparkling bottled flavoured water which may be more popular with younger people for example.

Socio- economic groups are important when considering press readership habits, the healthy qualities of our products may be worth advertising in publications dealing with such issues, and read by certain groups.

Psychological aspects are useful in segmentation because people of similar age and socio-economic background may lead very different lifestyles, individuals may have a value based on caution and therefore buy a safe reliable car. Likewise our products can be promoted as 'safe' to drink in many different situations.

Situational use concerns how people will buy the same product at different times for different uses. As such achieving customer loyalty is important, customers may be just thirsty, or in different circumstances having water with a meal. Targeting and maintaining the brand with these consumers is very important.

It is important if we are to run a successful cost effective campaign that we identify our most lucrative market segments and market accordingly.

Marketing campaign costs and brand value:

It is exciting to think that Valley Spring will expand into a new factory in the future and I understand your reasons for wishing to enhance the assets as shown on our statement of financial position. However accounting rules contained with international financial reporting standards, and specifically IAS 38 Intangible Assets will not allow either the marketing campaign costs or the value of the brand to be included in the statement of financial position. I will consider each element in turn.

Marketing campaign costs:

It could be argued that the cost of the marketing campaign does potentially meet the definition of an intangible asset because there has been a past event (the payment) which will generate future economic benefit that will flow to Valley Spring in terms of increased revenues in the future. Also there is no physical substance here and hence the benefits derived from the expenditure will be intangible in nature. Additionally the cost can be reliably measured because the payment for the campaign will be in the form of cash.

However, in order for expenditure to be capitalised as an intangible asset it must create an asset which is identifiable. This means that the asset can be separated out from the rest of the business and has arisen from contractual or other legal rights.

The easiest of these points to address is the point about contractual and legal rights. A marketing campaign in itself does not convene any contractual or other legal rights to external parties. Consumers might be encouraged to buy the new flavoured water as a result of the marketing (and therefore generate economic benefit for Valley Spring) but there is no contract or legally enforceable right which means that they are bound to buy the product. From Valley Spring's point of view there is no legal right to receive income from the campaign (in the form of sales) and therefore the campaign expenditure cannot be capitalised as an intangible asset.

The second point to address is that of being able to separate out the asset from the rest of the business. In effect this means that we could sell the intangible asset without selling the rest of the business. The whole purpose of the marketing campaign is that it will generate additional revenue in the future for the new flavoured water products. However we cannot sell this potential additional revenue stream to an external party without selling the products themselves, which clearly is not the intention.

Therefore as a result of all of this the expenditure on the marketing campaign cannot be capitalised in the statement of financial position and instead must be expensed to profit or loss as incurred.

Brand value:

The value of our Valley Spring brand does hold one of the characteristics which would allow it to be construed as an asset in that the strength of our brand does potentially increase our future revenues. However, there are a number of other characteristics which are not met, each of which is discussed below.

Firstly, to place a value on our brand is very subjective. Whilst there are various brand valuation methods and specialist consultants available to undertake such work, such a valuation is unlikely to meet the definition of reliable measurement required by the accounting standard. This is because of the large number of assumptions about the future which would be required.

Secondly, in order to capitalise the value of a brand, that brand needs to be either acquired from an external source (where there is therefore a reliable measurement base being the consideration paid) or be capable of separation from the rest of the business in the sense that it can be sold. In our case, clearly our brand value has been generated through internal means rather than as a result of an acquisition. In addition, if we were to separate our brand with a view to selling it then we would have nothing left in the business as we would no longer have the right to use the Valley Spring name. Also our brand strength is largely derived from our water source. Therefore in our case we could not sell the brand without selling the water source which in effect would mean us selling the whole business.

Therefore we cannot capitalise the value of our brand in the statement of financial position.

Exercise 3

Split of fixed and variable elements of direct production labour and energy costs and forecasting methods

<u>Direct production labour costs:</u>

In the short terms direct production labour is likely to be largely fixed in nature, which is contrary to how we currently treat such costs in our management information. This is because our workforce are likely to be contracted to work certain hours and hence we have a commitment to pay them for those hours, whether they are being productive or not. If for some reason we were unable to bottle water (for example, as a result of the spring being contaminated) then we would still need to pay our staff, certainly in the short term. Employment law will protect their contractual rights.

Any overtime that we pay for or any temporary labour that we employ can however be treated as a variable cost because these costs will only arise as a result of production.

Clearly in the longer term labour costs will be variable in nature, because we will be able to negotiate new terms of make staff redundant if needed.

In terms of better forecasting the split to establish our standard costs, it should be relatively straight forward to establish within our normal production how much of the cost relates to contracted hours (and therefore fixed) and how much arises from overtime and flexible temporary labour (and therefore variable). This proportion could then be used going forward, although would need to be reviewed if production changed such that either more or less overtime or temporary labour were being used.

<u>Energy:</u>

Energy is by far our largest production cost at 64% of the total production overhead. To date we have always treated this as a fixed cost, however a significantly proportion of the cost will be generated as a direct result of production in terms of running the machinery in the factory and hence is in fact variable in nature.

There will be a fixed element to the energy costs as there will be a base level of energy required to keep the factory operational, even when there is no production. However, the majority of the energy consumption will be directly linked to production.

In terms of better forecasting the split, it might be useful here to adopt a forecasting method known as the high-low method. This involves establishing cost data at just two points which are the highest level of activity and the lowest level of activity. So in respect of our energy cost we need to establish the cost at the point of zero production (which we could measure perhaps on a day at the weekend when there is no production) and then the cost at maximum production (which we could measure on a normal production day). We can then calculate the variable cost per batch of 1,000 bottles as the increase in the energy cost divided by the increase in number of batches of production. This can then be used to determine the total variable cost based on our maximum production, the reminder of the cost therefore being the fixed element.

Exercise 4

Report on the Implications of Expanding the Customer Base:

Purpose of Report:

The purpose of this report is to consider the implications of Valley Spring expanding the customer base from our current three large customers to include a number of small customers. The report will cover the following:

The practical impact of this on the finance function

The impact of supplying directly to small scale customers on the risks faced by Valley Spring

Any measures that Valley Spring could adopt to manage and mitigate any additional risk.

Practical Impact on the Finance Function:

An increase in the number of customers would significantly increase the administrative burden on the finance function. Additional staffing will be required in order to undertake the following tasks:

Order processing and invoice processing. The volume of transactions will increase significantly which potentially will put pressure on the finance function, unless appropriately staffed.

Monitoring of receivable balances and chasing up of any late payments. Again this could take considerable time.

More sophisticated computer systems may be required, involving a change in staff skills, investment in training and capital investment in the systems themselves.

Outsourcing the function may be worth considering if a sufficient level of transactions is reached. This will also mitigate some of the risk factors mentioned below.

Impact of expanding the customer base on the risks faced by Valley Spring:

The key risk associated with selling directly to small scale customers is that they either do not pay or pay very late. Due to their size this type of customer is more likely to have or to encounter cash flow difficulties than a large customer such as a supermarket. The implication of this for Valley Spring is two-fold:

It will affect our own cash flow position and potentially lead to issues with us paying our own suppliers.

It could have a direct impact on our profit if we have to write off receivable balances.

However, there is another risk impact in that by broadening our customer base it means that we become less reliant on individual customers. Currently we only have three customers. If for any reason we were to lose one of these then it would have a seriously damaging effect on the business in terms of revenue and cash flow. Broadening our customer base would potentially diversify some of this risk and therefore can be seen as a potentially positive impact. However, there is a negative aspect to this as well in that we do risk alienating our wholesale customer because they could consider us to be in direct competition with them, which could result in us losing their custom. It is unlikely that we would generate sufficient revenue from the new small customers to mitigate such a loss.

Measures that Valley Spring could adopt to manage additional risks:

There are a number of measures that we could adopt to manage the additional risks arising from selling directly to small scale customers.

Recruit appropriate qualified people for the finance department:

It would be sensible to recruit an appropriate experienced and qualified credit controller to ensure that all new customers are assessed as to their credit worthiness and that the receivables are monitored and chased for payment as required in a timely manner.

Ensure sound credit control procedures are established:

All potential customers should be assessed as to their creditworthiness prior to being accepted. This might involve purchasing credit agency reports or performing an internal assessment through looking at financial statements. In addition there should be procedures in place for the regular monitoring of outstanding debts and for chasing up late payments through telephone calls and letters.

Ensure that the credit terms given to the customer are appropriate:

Currently our customers are given 60 day credit terms. This is because as large scale customers they have demanded such terms. With any new small scale customers we should consider reducing this to a standard 30 days. This would certainly improve cash flow and would potentially limit the risk.

Financing of receivables through factoring:

Ultimately to protect against the risk of irrecoverable debt we could at a future date factor our receivables under a without recourse agreement. This would in effect mean that we would sell our outstanding debts to a finance company which would be responsible for recovering the monies and would take on the risk of recoverability. This would have the effect of immediately improving our cash flow, although it would be relatively expensive to implement.

Careful consideration of the position with the wholesale customer:

Lastly before any decision is made regarding selling to small scale customers, Valley Spring's relationship with our wholesale customer needs to be considered. You mention that the small scale customers who contacted you didn't currently sell our water. If all of the small scale customers that we took on were the same then this is likely to have a limited impact on our relationship with our wholesale customer. However, if small scale customers switch from them to us then this could be detrimental to retaining their business.

Feb. 2015 exam – variant 1 – debrief

Chapter learning objectives

- To gain a deeper understanding of how to write an answer that scores well in the real exam.

1 Introduction

As we have already explained in previous chapters the case study examinations are marked against a series of competencies. It is important that you understand this process to ensure you maximise your marks in the exam.

Once you have reviewed Chapter fifteen, attempted the February 2015 variant 1 exam and reviewed the suggested solutions this chapter takes you through the official marking guide, the examiner's feedback on student performance and contains some tutor tips to help you understand what the examiner is looking for.

2 Marking guide

The CIMA official marking guide for variant 1 of the Feb. 2015 exam is given as follows:

Section	Technical skills		Business skills		People skills		Leadership skills		Integration	Total
1	Dealing with constrained labour hours and throughput accounting	17	Factors to be considered and whether throughput would be beneficial	16						33
2	Captalisation of marketing costs and brand	14			Use of market segmentation in marketing campaign and communication	14				28
3	Cost behaviour for energy and labour costs, including forecasting methods	14								14
4	Impact of taking on small scale customers	16					Recommended actions	6	3	25
Total marks available for competency		61		16		14		6	3	100

The tasks can be mapped to the underlying papers and competences as follows:

	Designed to test ability to:	Competency being tested:	Syllabus learning outcome:
Section 1	Explain appropriate basis for a production decision concerning a short term constraint.	Technical skills	P1 – analyse short-term pricing and product decisions
	Demonstrate understanding of throughput accounting	Technical skills	P1 – discuss costing methods and their results
	Explain suitability of throughput to Valley Spring	Business skills	P1 – discuss costing methods and their results
Section 2	Explain of benefits of market segmentation to a marketing campaign	People skills	E1 – apply tools and techniques to formulate the organisation's marketing strategies, including the collection, analysis and application of big data
	Apply IAS 38 Intangible Assets with respect to brand value and marketing expenditure	Technical skills	F1 – produce the primary financial statements of an individual entity incorporating accounting transactions and adjustments, in accordance with the relevant international financial reporting standards, in an ethical manner
Section 3	Demonstrate understanding of cost behaviours and forecasting techniques	Technical skills	P1 – discuss costing methods and their results and prepare forecasts of financial results
Section 4	Explain the practical impact on the finance function of supplying to small scale customers	Business skills	E1 – Explain how the finance function supports the organisation's strategies and operations
	Explain the risks to the business of supplying to small scale customers	Technical skills	F1 – Evaluate the working capital position of an entity
	Describe actions that the business could take to mitigate these risks	Leadership skills	F1 – Evaluate the working capital position of an entity

3 Examiner's comments on the exam as a whole

After each sitting the examiners release their views and thoughts on the exam. This is what the examiner commented on the Feb. 2015 exam as a whole (i.e. not related to a specific variant):

This was the first sitting of the Operational level case study examination. Each of the five variants deployed assessed the core competencies of technical, business and people skills in the same proportions and proved to be very similar in terms of their overall difficulty, as demonstrated by the scores achieved. There was a broad range of performance on each of the five variants, with some excellent answers as well as a number of poor or incomplete answers. As expected, most answers were in the mid-range.

On the whole, candidates appeared to be prepared for the fact that each section of the variant had its own time element, with virtually all candidates completing answers for each section.

It was encouraging to see some attempt at application to the scenario of Valley Spring, especially in relation to the Enterprise pillar elements of the variants. Candidates who were able to link the scenario into their answers generally scored well.

However, this ability to apply knowledge to the scenario does still need to be developed, especially in relation to the Performance and Finance pillars. Answers which simply reproduced knowledge without application to the specific situation of Valley Spring scored few marks.

There was some evidence of rote-learned answers being reproduced in response to some of the tasks. Clearly there had been some question spotting, although such answers generally scored poorly as they were neither applied to the scenario nor answered the specific question asked.

Overall, the competency which was demonstrated the most was business skills, closely followed by people skills. This corresponds to the fact that candidates seemed better prepared to apply their Enterprise pillar knowledge to Valley Spring. Demonstration of technical skills was often mixed, which is disappointing given that there is a 64% weighting for this. It must be borne in mind that the Operational level case study examination is based upon all of the syllabi for P1, E1 and F1 and therefore candidates must be prepared for that.

There were three marks available for integration of knowledge within each variant. Candidates who commented around a subject area and brought in other relevant information from other subject areas or syllabi were awarded these marks.

4 Exam Section 1

Review of marking guide

The part of the marking guide that relates to this task is as follows:

Section	Technical skills		Business skills		People skills		Leadership skills		Integration	Total
1	Dealing with constrained labour hours and throughput accounting	17	Factors to be considered and whether throughput would be beneficial	16						33
Total marks available for competency		17		16						33

It is always worth reviewing marking guides to check that you are happy with the total marks and how the different tasks relate to the competences:

- The first section had a time allocation of 60 minutes, so is worth 33% of the marks

- Dealing with decision making under constraints is a technical aspect of the P1 syllabus, so earns technical skills marks

- The explanation of throughput accounting would be classified as technical skills whereas the discussion as to whether or not it would be beneficial to Valley Spring earns business skills marks.

Examiner's comments on student performance

The examiner's specific comments on performance on task 1 were as follows:

Section 1 on limiting factor analysis and throughput accounting was generally not well answered. Many answers were muddled and a number did not identify the fact that the direct production labour was in fact constrained. However, there was a significant minority that did correctly identify that production of the smaller bottles should take priority given the constraint in labour hours. Many candidates commented successfully on the removal of the constraint but few identified many other factors to be considered.

Answers on throughput accounting were very brief and superficial, with very few commenting on its suitability to the business.

The main conclusion to draw from this is that many students did not know their underlying P1 knowledge well enough for these topics.

Understanding the model answer

The first part of the task related to how best to make a decision in the circumstances described. Hopefully you remembered from P1 that the general rule is that we look at relevant cash flows for decision making. In many scenarios this equates to looking at contribution. In particular if we introduce the additional complication of scare resources, then we can rank different alternatives by looking at contribution per unit of scarce resource. Here that would suggest looking at contribution per direct labour hour.

Given this we can see that the model answer is structured as follows:

(1) Reasons why gross profit is not suitable

- it includes fixed costs – essentially an argument based on the concept of relevant costs, even though this term is not used

- context of constraint

- figure used for absorbed overhead is unsuitable

- conclusion

(2) Reasons why contribution is suitable

- it only includes what changes as a result of the decision – again an argument based on the concept of relevant costs

- explanation of how to incorporate the constraint

- application to Valley spring using illustrative numbers

(3) Other factors

- technique gives a commercially unacceptable solution – it suggests not selling one of the new products (Note: always be ready to appraise and criticise the output of any decision-making process)

- discussion of constraint – are labour hours really constrained or are there ways of getting round this?

- potential measurement issues

- other reasons why the result of the technical analysis may not give a commercially acceptable answer – existing sales orders.

The next sub-requirement looks at throughput accounting

(1) Basic explanation of throughput (Note: if you couldn't remember this when attempting task 1, maybe you should learn the examiner's version!)

   – link to MC and contribution

   – assumption that materials are the only variable cost

   – application to identifying and dealing with bottlenecks

(2) Application to Valley Spring

   – context – more than simply changing the costing system

   – discussion of bottlenecks and constraints – all of this is applied to VS rather than being discussed in general terms

   – context – less relevant to longer term decisions

5 Exam Section 2

Review of marking guide

The part of the marking guide that relates to this task is as follows:

Section	Technical skills		Business skills		People skills		Leadership skills		Integration	Total
2	Marketing costs and brand	14			Use of market segmentation in marketing campaign and communication	14				28
Total marks available for competency		14				14				28

It is always worth reviewing marking guides to check that you are happy with the total marks and how the different tasks relate to the competences:

- The first section had a time allocation of 50 minutes, so is worth 28% of the marks

- You may have been surprised to see that explaining the benefits of market segmentation to a marketing campaign would be considered people skills rather than business skills.

- The application of IAS 38 to brand value and marketing expenditure is classed as technical skills as expected.

Examiner's comments on student performance

The examiner's specific comments on performance on task 2 were as follows (emphasis added):

> Section 2 had mixed answers. Many candidates were able to discuss market segmentation and indeed there were many good answers where **relevant examples** were given which directly **related to the flavoured bottled water market**. The financial reporting issues surrounding the capitalisation of brand value and marketing costs was less well answered, with many candidates concluding incorrectly that both could be capitalised. Those candidates who were able to **apply** the definition of an asset to marketing costs and brand value scored highly.

The key lesson to draw from this is the need to apply comments and discussion to the specific circumstances of the company concerned.

Understanding the model answer

The first part of the task related to market segmentation. As mentioned above, the key here is to relate your comments to the specific circumstances of Valley Spring.

The model answer is structured as follows:

(1) Introduction

- definition of segmentation – note that even here the examiner relates the answer back to Valley Spring

- why we bother with segmentation – different groups have different needs

(2) Methods of segmentation and targeting

- Basic idea – e.g. cost effective campaign

- Example applied to Valley Spring – young v old

- Example applied to Valley Spring – geographical

- Example applied to Valley Spring – family lifecycle

- Example applied to Valley Spring – socio-economic

- Example applied to Valley Spring – psychological

- Example applied to Valley Spring – situational

(3) Desirable properties of segments

- "Measurable" + two examples applied to Valley Spring

- "Accessible" + application to Valley Spring

- "Substantial" + example applied to Valley Spring

(4) Application to Valley Spring – Marketing strategy

- Example applied to Valley Spring – demographic
- Example applied to Valley Spring – incomes
- Example applied to Valley Spring – socio-economic
- Example applied to Valley Spring – psychological
- Example applied to Valley Spring – situational

Note: The key lesson to learn here is that the bulk of the answer consists of discussing how the concepts apply to Valley Spring!

The second part of the task related to capitalisation of costs. In many respects the structure of the answer is more obvious as it involves applying the financial accounting rules

(1) Introduction

- Context
- Statement of conclusion – cannot capitalise costs

(2) Marketing campaign costs

- Discussion of intangible asset – past event – applied to marketing costs
- Discussion of intangible asset – lack of physical substance – applied to marketing costs
- Discussion of intangible asset – costs can be measured – applied to marketing costs
- Discussion of capitalisation – identifiable
- Discussion of capitalisation – contractual and legal rights – applied to marketing costs
- Discussion of capitalisation – ability to separate out asset – applied to marketing costs
- Conclusion

(3) Brand

- Brand does increase future revenues
- Discussion of subjectivity of valuation methods
- Discussion of whether acquired or generated internally
- Discussion of whether capable of separation – e.g. could it be sold?
- Conclusion

Note: the key lesson to learn here is the importance of knowing the technical content.

6 Exam Section 3

Review of marking guide

The part of the marking guide that relates to this task is as follows:

Section	Technical skills		Business skills	People skills	Leadership skills		Integration	Total
3	Cost behaviour for energy and labour costs, including forecasting methods	14						14
Total marks available for competency		14						14

It is always worth reviewing marking guides to check that you are happy with the total marks and how the different tasks relate to the competences:

- Section 3 had a time allocation of 25 minutes, so is worth 14% of the marks

- Dealing with cost behaviour and forecasting are technical aspects of the P1 syllabus, so earns technical skills marks.

Examiner's comments on student performance

The examiner's specific comments on performance on task 3 were as follows:

> Again in section 3 answers were varied, although often those that scored poorly had written very little. Within the single task for this section, the second bullet point asked for how the split of the fixed and variable elements of the cost might be better forecasted and those that specifically discussed forecasting methods scored well.

The main conclusion to draw from this is that many students did not know their underlying P1 knowledge well enough for these topics and failed to develop points by applying them to Valley Spring.

Understanding the model answer

The first part of the task related to whether costs were fixed or variable. The concept here is very straightforward. However, key to a good answer was in discussing the specific circumstances of Valley Spring.

Given this we can see that the model answer is structured as follows:

(1) Direct production labour costs

– Short term – significant element fixed due to contracted hours

– Overtime variable

– Long term – variable due to ability to reduce staff numbers

– Discussion of implications for forecasting with significant application to Valley Spring

(2) Energy

– Context – treated as fixed

– Discussion – some aspects fixed, others variable

– Discussion of implications for forecasting with significant application to Valley Spring

The key lesson here is the need to apply points to the scenario given.

7 Exam Section 4

Review of marking guide

The part of the marking guide that relates to this task is as follows:

Section	Technical skills		Business skills		People skills		Leadership skills		Integration	Total
4	Impact of taking on small scale customers	16					Recommended actions	6	3	25
Total marks available for competency		16						6	3	25

It is always worth reviewing marking guides to check that you are happy with the total marks and how the different tasks relate to the competences:

- This section had a time allocation of 45 minutes, so is worth 25% of the marks

- The impact on the finance function is a technical aspect of the F1 syllabus, so earns technical skills marks

- Recommendations earn leadership marks

- Integration marks are earned by stepping back and seeing the bigger picture – how would taking on small customers impact on wholesale customers.

Examiner's comments on student performance

The examiner's specific comments on performance on task 4 were as follows:

> The answers in section 4 were on the whole encouraging with many candidates scoring well. Most identified that the main issue would be the increase in the number of transactions and the pressure this would place on the finance function. The risks were also well understood, both in terms of the risks themselves and measures to mitigate them. There was some very good application demonstrated in this section.

The main conclusion to draw from this is that many students did know their underlying F1 knowledge and applied it well.

Understanding the model answer

The first thing to recognise is that you have been asked for a report so an introduction would be required.

The whole task relates to managing smaller customers – firstly the practical impact on the finance function of supplying directly to small scale customers, next the impact on the risks faced by Valley Spring of supplying directly to small scale customers; and finally any measures that Valley Spring could adopt to manage and mitigate any additional risks. All of these relate to technical aspects of F1 and E1 and some common sense. Key to a good answer lies in applying comments to the scenario.

Given this we can see that the model answer is structured as follows:

(1) Introduction

- purpose of report

(2) Practical aspects

- Increased admin – order and invoice processing
- Increased admin – credit control
- Impact on MIS
- Outsourcing?

(3) Impact on risks

- Potential negative impact – non or late payment – impact on cash and profit
- Potential positive impact – less reliant on existing customers
- Potential negative impact – reaction of existing customers.

(4) Potential solutions

- Recruit experienced staff
- Implement credit control procedures
- Implement appropriate credit terms
- Factoring
- Impact on wholesale customers

Key to the examiner's answer is the degree of application to the specific circumstances of Valley Spring.

8 Integration

There are 3 integration marks available in the exam. Here they have been taken out of the technical marks in task 4 and relate to discussing the bigger picture.

9 Summary

You should now have a better understanding of what a good answer looks like and how to achieve one.

Next steps:

(1) Revisit any technical aspects that you found tricky.

(2) Given you are "up to speed 11 with Valley Spring, it would be worthwhile practicing further cases, so go on the CIMA website and download the unseen exams for variants 2, 3, 4 and 5 to attempt.

(3) Await the 'live' pre-seen for your exam.

(4) Re-perform the suggestions in this textbook using the real pre-seen to ensure you are prepared for the exam.

(5) Consider choosing a study option which gives you access to practice mocks – an important stage in your exam preparation.

17

Feedback on the real exam and tips on answering the more technical aspects of P1 and F1

Chapter learning objectives

To understand how to answer exam tasks that focus on the more technical areas of F1 and P1.

1 Summary of exams to date

1.1 Topic coverage

At the time of printing this text, we have had 7 sittings of the real exam, each with five variants of four sections (tasks), giving 140 tasks.

While these cover the full range of the syllabi of the underlying papers, it is possible to identify certain topics that have cropped up more than others:

P1

- Activity based costing – e.g. explaining the benefits of switching to ABC
- Relevant costing – e.g. applying the principles of relevant costing to a shut-down decision
- Variance statements – e.g. explaining causes of key variances
- Pay-off tables and decision making under uncertainty

F1

- Capitalising costs – e.g. brand, marketing costs, research costs
- Tangible non-current assets – e.g. which costs can be capitalised, treatment of disposals
- Receivables management
- Accounting for associate/subsidiary

E1

- Marketing strategies – e.g. marketing mix for new product
- Reward schemes and performance related pay
- Sourcing strategies – e.g. inhouse v outsourcing, single v multiple, choice of suppliers
- Quality – e.g. costs of quality, benefits of implementing TQM

Note: Any topic from F1, P1 and E1 could come up in your real exam – it is vital that you are prepared for anything!

1.2 Examiner's feedback

After each exam sitting CIMA publish the exams, suggested answers, summary marking guides and an examiner's report that discusses all five variants from that sitting.

While many students are producing high quality scripts in the time available, there are common themes that have arisen where students can improve. Here are some typical comments:

- **Time pressure is not the main problem**

  "There was little evidence that time pressure caused any problems and most candidates completed answers for all tasks, although in some of the variants answers on specific elements of tasks were superficial or too brief... Often this seemed to be due to a lack of technical knowledge..." (Feb 2016)

- **No need for lengthy introductions**

  "Some candidates are wasting time giving extraneous information. There were often lengthy introductions to issues given which then meant that there was less time to address the actual task in hand. There are no marks for introductions or setting the scene; candidates need to address the task being asked and no more." (Feb 2016)

- **Planning answers is important**

  "When sitting an Operational level case study examination, it is important to take time to plan your answer so that you are able to apply your knowledge to the specifics of the case. I would suggest that for certain tasks you plan your answers in the answer screen itself.

  For example, if you are asked for the potential benefits and problems of outsourcing a particular function, I would suggest that you first note down headings for benefits and problems. Then under each heading list your benefits and problems; these will become your sub-headings. Then you can write a short paragraph under each sub-heading.

  This will allow you time to think about all of the points that you want to make and will help to give your answer a clear format. Ultimately, it should save you time". (Feb 2016)

- **Apply models to the scenario**

   "There was evidence in a number of the variants of the erroneous use of learned models. In a case study the most important thing to do is to answer the task asked within the context of the business. The random inclusion of models such as Porter's value chain, with no application to First Class Bakery, earned no marks." (Feb 2016)

- **Justify comments made**

   "Candidates also need to be conscious of unsupported assertions. Making statements such as, "this improves decision making", "this graph is essential" or "planning is enhanced" is not enough to gain any marks. Candidates must explain "how" the model or technique achieves these assertions. Wild enthusiasm is not enough without sound and reasoned explanation. As in November many candidate answers would have been improved if they added "because of ...." at the end of a sentence to explain why something is as it is." (Feb 2016)

- **Technical marks for P1 and F1 are often the biggest discriminator**

   "As is consistent with other exam sessions, the skill which was demonstrated the best was business skills, closely followed by people skills. Candidates seemed to be most comfortable using their knowledge from E1 to demonstrate applied business and people skills. Applying knowledge from P1 and especially F1 to demonstrate technical skills appeared to be more challenging." (Feb 2016)

   "Application to the scenario was generally good for tasks that linked to the E1 and P1 syllabi but often still poor in relation to F1 and the more technical aspects of P1." (Feb 2016)

2 The marginally competent student

During 2016 CIMA disclosed further information on how the pass mark is set.

The process

A detailed process was revealed that involves the following:

(1) A panel of experts debate the tasks within a variant to decide what should be expected from a student deemed competent for this task. This debate does not focus on a perfect answer but, instead, asks what would be expected of a CIMA student (or member) in practice – what is the minimum expected if we were considering employing them, for example.

(2) A sample of student scripts is then discussed and the scripts ranked. This is repeated and refined until the "marginally competent student" is identified. This student deserves to pass (but only just!) as they would be employable and have the skills expected of a CIMA student or member in the real world.

(3) The marks earned by this script are then used to set the pass mark and standardise the overall marking system. Amoungst other things, this ensures that students are not disadvantaged if they sit a "harder" variant.

The lessons to be learned

When answering a task in the exam, you could imagine that this was part of a job interview and ask yourself what would be required to get the job.

Your employer would be less impressed by you showing off knowledge but much more impressed that you can answer a question set, apply your comments to the company's specific circumstances and make practical, relevant suggestions.

Make sure your answers do this!

3 Answering more technical aspects of P1

3.1 Introduction

As stated above, one of the main differentiators between students who pass and students who fail is answering the more technical aspects of F1 and P1.

In the next two sections we consider some examples of such tasks from the February 2016 exam.

3.2 The February 2016 exam

The pre-seen information for the February 2016 exam concerned a company called First Class Bakery (FCB), a cake and dessert manufacturer in the country of Beeland.

Key details were as follows:

- All products were currently sold within Beeland.

- Originally set up by three brothers, the company was now 20% owned by the one remaining brother, Frank Mitchell, who was also the MD, and 80% owned by Universal Foods, a large quoted group.

- First Class Bakery made three types of cake – slab cakes, special occasion cakes and desserts. Each went through three production processes – ingredient prep, mixing and baking and finishing – although the degree of labour involved depended on the product line.

- First Class Bakery had a good reputation for quality and VFM, although the bulk of its cakes were sold to large retailers with customers' own brand labels attached.

- Sales and profits fell in 2015, which was expected to some degree due to a declining market. However, in the case of First Class Bakery this also resulted in a considerable worsening of its cash position from cash in hand of B$870,000 at the start of the year to an overdraft of B$385,000 at the end.

- The company was also under-investing in non-current assets and seeing an increase in cash tied up in working capital.

Taking all these factors together, it could be argued that First Class Bakery was in serious need of new ideas to turn its fortunes around.

3.3 Variant 1 – section 4 – decision making under uncertainty

Scenario

- The company decided to bring out a new organic cherry slabcake.

- Four different contracts were being considered for the supply of the cherries from a new supplier called TOCC.

- Students were given a pay-off table and a regret table for each contract under three different demand projections.

Task

Students were asked to produce the following:

(1) An interpretation of the information included in the pay-off table

(2) An explanation of the Maximax, Maximin and Minimax Regret decision making criteria, including commentary on the risk attitudes of managers who employ such methods and identification of which contract would be selected under each of these decision criteria.

(3) An explanation of expected values and the potential benefits and problems of their use in the decision regarding the purchase of organic cherries.

Suggested answer approach/structure

Set up headings as suggested by the question requirement.

1. Interpretation of the pay-off table

- Start with *technical knowledge* – explain what a pay-off table shows but keep this part brief. Comments could include:

  "The pay-off table shows a measure of the value or 'pay-off' of each possible outcome in terms of the decision facing the directors."

  "A pay-off table can be a useful way to represent and analyse a scenario where there is a range of possible outcomes and responses."

  "A pay-off table illustrates all possible gains/losses and as such is often used in decision-making under conditions of uncertainty."

- Then *apply* this to FCB using the actual figures and scenario given. This is the most important aspect:

  "In our case there are four possible purchase levels for cherries from TOCC and there are three possible levels of demand from the customers."

  "The pay-off table shows the level of contribution that would be earned by First Class Bakery as a result of entering each of the alternative contracts depending on the level of demand from customers. The level of contribution would vary according to the contract size chosen."

- Try to *develop* points further by considering wider issues, implications and so on.

  "The price of organic cherries reduces as the contract size increases and therefore the contribution per cake would increase."

  "In situations where the contract size is greater than the level of customer demand then surplus cakes will be sold to local farmers."

- Developing your answer could also include judgement/scepticism/limitations of the method – for example,

  "The value of the table is very much dependent on the accuracy of the market research that has been undertaken."

2. Explanation of Maximax, Maximin and Minimax Regret

- For each method plan an approach, starting with technical knowledge and then applying to FCB.

  One such plan could be as follows:

  (1) Explain basic approach

  (2) Explain the underlying assumption

  (3) Link to risk attitudes

  (4) What decision should FCB make?

- Applying this to Maximax, for example, gives the following:

  Technical knowledge:

  Basic approach – "The Maximax rule to decision making involves selecting the decision option that would maximise the maximum pay-off potentially achievable."

  Underlying assumption – "It is based on the assumption that the best pay-off will occur."

  Link to risk attitudes – "This approach to decision making would be appropriate for a decision maker who has an optimistic approach to decision making and is prepared to select the decision option that would yield the best results if the most beneficial decision outcome were to occur."

  Application to FCB – decision backed up with data specific to the scenario:

  "Under the Maximax decision criterion Contract D would be selected since it might result in the highest possible contribution of B$744,000"

  This can then be repeated for the other two methods.

3. Explanation of expected values.

- The use of EVs:

  "The expected value is calculated by weighting each of the contribution levels by its associated probability.

  The sum of these weighted amounts is called the expected value of the probability distribution.

  In other words the expected value is the weighted arithmetic mean of the possible outcomes"

- Potential benefits:

  "Expected values are associated with risk neutrality and consider the probability of each possible outcome.

  The decision information is reduced to and represented by a single number that facilitates decision making.

  The calculations are relatively straightforward."

- Potential problems:

  "The probabilities used are usually very subjective because two individuals will not necessarily assign the same probabilities to a particular outcome.

  The expected value is merely a weighted average and therefore has little relevance for a one-off decision.

  The expected value does not necessarily correspond to any of the actual possible outcomes as in this decision".

Examiner's comments

Most of task 4 was reasonably well answered.

Interpreting the information in the payoff table was not well answered though. Many answers were brief and indeed a significant number of candidates missed it altogether. It would appear that candidates think that this is more complicated than it actually is.

A candidate who commented that there were four contracts being considered (each with a different purchase price for the cherries), that there were three possible levels of demand (hence uncertainty) and that each of the cells represented the contribution from each contract under each of the possible levels of demand, would have scored at least half marks. Those that commented about the fact that the contract choice was the decision and that the possible demand levels were outside of managements control, as well as commenting about the impact of the cherry price on contribution would have scored more marks again.

The explanation of the decision using maximax, maximin and minimax regret was well answered: candidates seem well prepared for this and many scored full marks. Most candidates were able to comment on expected value well but often the benefits and problems were only superficially addressed.

3.4 Variant 3 – section 4 – break even analysis including a graph

Scenario

- The company decided to bring out a new range of Gluten Absent (GA) products.

- Directors concerned about risk – especially whether the new products will break even.

- Students were given a multi-product break even chart with supporting tables of information.

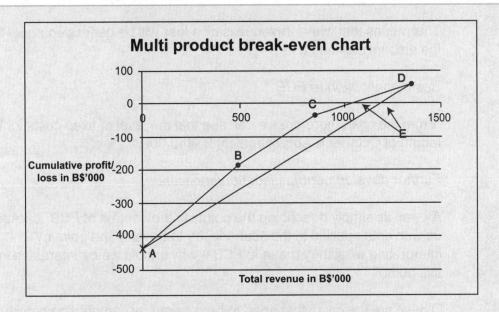

Task

Students were then asked to explain the following:

(1) What various points on the graph represented and what the two main lines were

(2) The usefulness of the chart to FCB.

Note: there was a third aspect to the task that looked at working capital management but we will focus on the P1 aspects here.

Suggested answer approach/structure

Set up headings as suggested by the question requirement.

1. Interpretation of the chart

*   Based on your technical knowledge you should be able to understand what each point represented. As well as explaining this, you would need to apply your comments to FCB by incorporating actual figures and details from the chart given in the scenario.

*   For example, point A was where there were zero sales. Comments could include:

Technical knowledge:

"Point A is the point at which there is no revenue, where sales volumes are nil.

At this point fixed costs will still be incurred because by their very nature these costs are incurred regardless of production or activity levels.

This means that where revenue is nil a loss will be generated equal to the amount of fixed costs. "

Basic application to FCB

"From the chart therefore we can see that the level of fixed costs for the month of October is approximately B$440,000."

Further development/justification/implications

As well as simply describing the points in the context of FCB, backed up with data specific to the scenario, try to develop the point by interpreting what they mean to FCB – why should we be interested in this point?

"These are the costs that need to be covered by contribution before a profit can be made."

- Similarly, point(s) E represented break-even:

Technical knowledge:

"Point E is the break-even point on each line."

Basic application:

"Looking at the chart one can see that the break-even point (the point at which neither a profit nor a loss is expected to be made) on the straight line is where revenue is approximately B$1,225,000.

Further development

Here we can do more to interpret what the figures mean to FCB

"This means that revenue can fall to this level from the expected level of B$1,356,000 before we reach the point where fixed costs are not covered by contribution."

- Next you had to comment on why there were two lines

This was harder as you needed to recognise that one line assumed selling products in constant mix but the other allowed us to sell in the order of highest C/S ratio.

"The line between points A and D represents the expected profit or loss at different revenue levels assuming that the mix of sales that we expect is kept the same regardless of the level of total revenue."

"In other words each point on the line represents sales revenue being comprised of 37% from sales of lemon cakes, 34% from sales of carrot cakes and 29% from sales of coffee cakes."

"The line which connects points A, B, C and D is the line that represents the relationship between revenue and profit or loss on the assumption that we sell the cakes in order of profitability (measured as the c/s ratio)."

- Note that the answer here is applied to the scenario. Indeed it could have been expanded further to give the order in which the cakes were assumed to be sold (carrot, coffee and then lemon).

2. The usefulness of this multi-product break-even chart

- Make sure you consider both sides of the argument and try to justify/develop points.
- For example, when arguing that the chart is useful, you could develop your argument as follows:

Technical knowledge:

"The chart is useful because it gives an idea of the level of revenue at which we will make neither a profit nor a loss."

Application:

"This is particularly relevant in our case because these are new products in what is a new and specialised market for us and therefore we do not have experience at forecasting sales volumes."

Development:

"The sales team have given their best estimates for the month of October, but there is no past experience to base this on, which means that its accuracy is questionable."

Examiner's comments

In the first element of task 4 most candidates made a sensible attempt at explaining each of the points A, B, C, D and E and most were able to identify A as the fixed costs (although many did not state what those fixed costs were from the chart).

There was some confusion on the other points however (especially points B and C), although some candidates did achieve full marks here.

Many candidates were not able to comment on the differences between the two lines.

Answers in respect of the usefulness of break-even in this situation were mixed. Most did not comment that a margin of safety could be established and the majority of answers were very generic.

3.5 Variant 4 – section 1 – linear programming, including a graph

Scenario

- The company was negotiating a large order with a major customer.

- If successful, then production capacity would be expanded in the long term. However, in the short term (the next 3 months) the company had to deal with a number of constraints. These were described but not given in mathematical terms.

- Students were given a linear programming graph (with various lines labelled), along with various equations and supporting tables of information.

Task

Students were then asked to prepare a briefing note that:

(1) Interpreted the linear programming graph

(2) Explained the usefulness of the graph to FCB.

Suggested answer approach/structure

This would have been very tricky had you forgotten basic technical knowledge concerning linear programming! As stated earlier, no topics are off-limits to the examiner.

1. Interpretating the graph

- Planning your approach is more critical here than in some other requirements as there are many components to linear programming that need to be incorporated.

  With the break-even chart covered in the previous section the requirement specifically asked for comments on each labelled point on the chart. Here it doesn't explicitly ask that but it would wise to incorporate such explanations in your answer and identify what each line represents.

  Linear programming has a well defined series of steps, so a very good approach (and structure) would be to walk through the method:

  (1) identify/explain constraints,

  (2) identify/explain the feasible region,

  (3) identify/explain the objective function/iso-contribution line,

  (4) identify the optimal solution and interpret.

- Based on your technical knowledge you should be able to link the narrative concerning constraints with the equations given and hence identify which line represents which constraint.

"Each line on the graph represents a potential constrained resource to our production of the new dessert flavours: line A relates to unrefined sugar, line B to labour hours, line C to machine hours and line D to demand for the coffee and walnut flavour."

"Each of the lines A, B and C represents the different combinations of production of x (batches of organic chocolate) and y (batches of coffee and walnut) that will utilise all of the resource and hence represents the maximum production under each resource."

"Line D is a demand constraint line."

- With the different steps in linear programming, you can give a general comment based on technical knowledge and then apply to the scenario. For example, considering the idea of the feasible region:

Technical knowledge:

"In order to interpret the graph we need to identify the 'feasible region' of production. The feasible region is the area on the graph contained within all of the constraint lines (which are lines A, B, C and D). In situations where there are several constraints (as in this case), the feasible region will be the area below each of the lines that is common to all constraints."

"The reason the feasible region is below the lines and not above the lines is because these lines represent the maximum production or demand of x and y given the constraint in place, hence it is only possible to have production below the line and not above it."

Basic application

"In our graph, the feasible region (which remember is the area below each line which is common to all) is the area below both line C and line D, which means that line C (the machine hours constraint) and line D (the sales volume for coffee and walnut desserts constraint) are our binding constraints."

Further development/explanation

"The optimum solution for the production of organic chocolate and coffee and walnut desserts must therefore be in this feasible area, because it is only at production within this area that we will have enough machine hours and demand for the coffee and walnut desserts."

2. The usefulness of the linear programming graph

- Make sure you consider both sides of the argument and try to justify/develop points.

- For example, when arguing that the approach is useful, you could develop your argument as follows:

Technical knowledge:

"The linear programming graph is a useful tool in situations like this where there are a number of potential resource constraints on production, as it does identify the optimum solution where contribution will be maximised within the boundaries of the constraints."

Application:

"In our case: production of 200 batches of coffee and walnut and 180 batches of organic chocolate."

Development

Given this is an argument, make sure you consider counter arguments/limitations and so on:

"However, whilst this is the production plan that in theory maximises contribution, this ignores other factors such as customer requirements."

"Also, a linear programming solution is only ever sensible for a very short term production decision or within a small range of production. This is because over time and volumes the nature of costs can change, Linear programming works on the assumption of linearity, and therefore ignores changes over time and economies of scale."

Examiner's comments

> Task 1 was the most poorly answered part of this variant.
>
> Few candidates appeared to be familiar with linear programming; indeed many confused it with either linear regression or breakeven analysis. This is quite worrying as this subject should have been learned while studying P1.
>
> For those candidates that did interpret the linear programming graph, the majority noted that lines A, B, C, D represented the constraints. However, only a few candidates noted that the binding constraints were represented by lines C and D. There was little attempt to explain the feasible region, the iso-contribution line or to conclude about the optimal solution. Few candidates produced anything but the most superficial analysis and therefore scored very poorly.
>
> In the second element of the task two things are worthy of note. Firstly, if asked to explain how useful a model is to a business, the analysis should include a balanced argument, otherwise how can its usefulness be assessed? Most candidates only considered the benefits of linear programming. Secondly, stating "it is very useful "is not enough, even if this is qualified by "as it will improve management decision making". To get a good mark a candidate needs to explain how management decision making is improved.

4 Answering more technical aspects of F1

4.1 Introduction

As stated above, one of the main differentiators between students who pass and students who fail is answering the more technical aspects of F1 and P1.

In the last section we considered some P1 tasks from the February 2016 exam. Here we look at some F1 tasks that caused particular difficulties for candidates.

4.2 Variant 2 – section 4 – group accounting

Scenario

- FCB had an opportunity to buy shares in Home Style Bakery, a bespoke cake manufacturer.

- The precise number of shares on offer was unclear – it could be anything between 20% and 80%.

Task

Students were asked to produce briefing notes on the following:

(1) The factors to be considered when deciding whether the investment in Home Style Bakery would be a trade investment, associate or subsidiary.

(2) How this classification would impact the profit and loss, assuming group accounts are prepared. Frank was particularly keen to understand the impact on revenue.

Suggested answer approach/structure

Set up headings as suggested by the question requirement.

1. Factors to be considered

- A common problem with more detailed financial reporting tasks is that students fail to incorporate all the factors they should but focus on just the main one or two. Given this, it is worth planning the key sub-headings that should come out of your technical knowledge.

  Deciding whether an investment is an associate or subsidiary (or neither) depends on the degree of **control/influence** FCB would have, which in turns depends on a range of factors, such as:

  (1) % shareholding,

  (2) voting rights,

  (3) board representation,

  (4) the relative power of other shareholders and so on.

  This could form the basis of an answer structure.

- Start with technical knowledge. Comments could include:

"When determining the type of investment for consolidation purposes the key consideration is whether we will have control over the operating and financing decisions that Home Style Bakery makes. If First Class Bakery has control over these decisions or the power to control these decisions, the investment will be a subsidiary.

If instead First Class Bakery has significant influence over the decisions of Home Style Bakery then this will mean that the investment will be an associate.

If there is neither the power to control nor significant influence over decisions then this will be a simple trade investment."

- Then apply this to FCB using the actual figures and scenario given. Our shareholding could be 20%, 40%, 60%, 80% or 100%. This is the most important aspect:

"Whether there is control or significant influence depends on the following factors:

The percentage investment in the equity shares of Home Style Bakery and the proportion of voting rights held.

In this instance we know that each equity share carries equal voting rights. Typically control will be gained where more than 50% of these rights are held and significant influence where 20% are held. In our case there is some uncertainty over the level of investment – it could be 20%, 40%, 60%, 80% or 100%.

The representation on the Board of directors.

In the case of Home Style Bakery each director has a 20% stake, and therefore it seems sensible to assume that each 20% block acquired will result in a director's post. At a 60% investment and 3 out of 5 of the directors this would give us the power to control and hence at 60% or above the investment is likely to be a subsidiary.

The power or influence of other shareholders.

If we have a 20% stake, given there will still be four of the original directors then it is likely that we won't even have significant influence. However at 40% with two out of five directors, it is more likely to be significant influence and hence an associate."

2. Impact on profit and loss

- For each classification, start with technical knowledge and then apply comments to FCB. As with P1 topics discussed previously, try to move beyond the obvious basic application into further implications. For example, when discussing a subsidiary:

  Technical knowledge:

  "If a subsidiary, then acquisition accounting will apply."

  Basic application to FCB:

  "This means that 100% of Home Style Bakery's income and expenses will be included with First Class Bakery."

  Further development/implications:

  "Any inter-company trade would then be eliminated".

  "If less than 100% of Home Style Bakery is acquired, the share of profit that relates to the non-controlling interests will be shown underneath the statement of profit or loss."

- Similar discussions can be done for associates and trade investments.
- In respect of revenue, the main challenge lies in having and applying technical knowledge:

  "only a subsidiary will increase this figure because we will include all of the subsidiaries revenue with ours. None of the other category of investment will affect the revenue figure"

Examiner's comments

Most candidates focused on the percentage of shares that may be purchased and the effect each would have on the classification of any investment in Home Style Bakery. Very few answers mentioned voting rights, representation on the board or the power of other shareholders. All of these can also have an impact on the classification of an investment.

Very few answers referred to the current share holdings and the effect different acquisitions would have. A significant proportion of candidates were not able to explain the consequences of the proposed acquisition on First Class Bakery's statement of profit or loss

4.3 Variant 3 – section 2 – research and development

Scenario

- The company decided to bring out a new range of Gluten Absent (GA) products.

- A table of development costs was given regarding investigating and developing recipes and baking processes.

Task

Students were then asked to explain how the expected expenditure should be treated in the financial statements.

Note: there was another aspect to the task that looked at just-in-time systems but we will focus on the F1 aspects here.

Suggested answer approach/structure

- As stated before, a common problem with more detailed financial reporting tasks is that students fail to incorporate all the factors they should and their answers lack structure. Planning is thus essential.

  Often with such tasks you will need to set up the answer structure based on the rules within the relevant accounting standard, so it is vital that you still know the level of detail required.

- Based on your F1 technical knowledge, you should recognise that we are looking at how to account for research and development costs. Given this, there are three key questions:

  (1) Is the expenditure linked to a research project or a development project?

  (2) If the project is a development project do we met the conditions to be able to capitalise the expenditure? This is where the detailed rules come into play.

  (3) What expenditure can be capitalised? One would expect to conclude that some of the planned expenditure could be capitalised but not all of it. The markers will be looking for a reasoned argument with justified points here.

- This could form the basis of your plan and, therefore, answer structure.

1. Is the expenditure linked to a research project or a development project?

- When applying accounting standards it is always worth starting with a basic statement of the relevant rule or principle.

  "The distinction between research and development expenditure is important because it determines whether the expenditure might be capitalised (development expenditure) or whether it must be expensed to profit or loss straight away (research expenditure)."

- Then apply the concept/rules FCB

  "In our case, this is development expenditure because the result of the project is a new range of gluten free products which it is intended to bring to the market as soon as the production facility is built. There is a potential intangible asset, in the form of the knowledge gained in the development of the recipes for the GA cakes, which is expected to generate future economic benefit."

2. If the project is a development project do we met the conditions to be able to capitalise the expenditure?

- To create the detailed structure within this section you need to remember that development expenditure can only be capitalised as an intangible asset if a number of criteria have been met. Each of these criteria can be set up as a sub-heading as follows:

  (1) It is technically feasible to complete the intangible asset so that it can be used.

  (2) It is intended to complete the intangible asset so that it can be used.

  (3) The business has the ability to use the intangible asset.

  (4) The intangible asset is expected to generate future economic benefit.

  (5) The resources exist to complete the intangible asset.

  (6) The expenditure attributable to the intangible asset can be reliably measured.

- Under each sub-heading (which are the six rules above), you would need to state the rule and then discuss whether or not it has been met and why.

  It is not enough to say a rule has been met without any explanation or justification!

- For example, rule 1:

  Technical knowledge – statement of rule

  "It is technically feasible to complete the intangible asset so that it can be used."

  Application with justification

  "In our case the recipes and baking process that we are developing are the intangible asset and it is likely that from early in the project this criteria will have been met **because** we will have had the expertise and experience within the team to create the end recipes".

- For example, rule 5:

  Technical knowledge – statement of rule

  "The resources exist to complete the intangible asset."

  Application with justification

  "Again from the start of the project there was always an intention to develop products which would be sold and **therefore** resources would have been made available."

- Finally with this section, recognise that, having evaluated each rule, you will need some form of conclusion:

  "So, it is likely that all of these criteria have been met at some point during the progress of the project. The key thing to establish is the point at which all of these criteria were satisfied, because from that date, development expenditure incurred should be capitalised."

3. What expenditure can be capitalised?

- Next you needed to look at the anticipated expenditure on a line by line basis and explain the accounting treatment. If you feel that it would not qualify as development expenditure, then how would it be treated – an expense or would it be capitalised for other reasons?

- For example:

  "There are two items on the schedule provided by Tony Swift which are not development expenditure:

  (1) B$50,000 has been spent on new equipment within the new product development kitchen. These are tangible assets of the business which will be used on future development projects and as such are not part of the development expenditure. Instead B$50,000 will be included as an addition to property, plant and equipment (PPE) in the statement of financial position.

  As with any other PPE, these assets will need to be depreciated over their useful economic life. The depreciation charge will reduce the carrying value of the assets in the statement of financial position. Usually the depreciation charge will also reduce profit, however in this instance it is possible that some of this depreciation charge can be included as part of development costs.

  (2) There is B$30,000 of general overhead included. This cannot be included as part of development expenditure in accordance with IAS 38 because this is an allocation of the general overhead and not a cost directly incurred as a result of the development. It should be expensed to profit and loss."

Examiner's comments

The second element of this task was not well done. Yet again, it would appear the knowledge of financial reporting standards is generally poor, let alone application to a specific issue.

In this case marks were available for commenting on the differences between research and development expenditure and the criteria that have to be met to capitalise development expenditure. Good candidates commented on each of the criteria in light of the situation at First Class Bakery (these were very few in number).

Many candidates though did correctly identify the new equipment as an IAS 16 issue.

4.5 Variant 4 – section 3 – accounting for brands

Scenario

- The company has increased its range of desserts and won new customers.

- One implication of this is the increased value of the FCB brand.

- Some directors want to reflect this value in the financial statements .

Task

Students were then asked to prepare a section of a report that explains the reasons why IFRSs prevent the inclusion of the brand within the financial statements.

Note: there was another aspect that looked at variances but we will focus on the F1 aspects here.

Suggested answer approach/structure

- As stated before, a common problem with more detailed financial reporting tasks is that students fail to incorporate all the factors they should and their answers lack structure. Planning is thus essential.

  Often with such tasks you will need to set up the answer structure based on the rules within the relevant accounting standard, so it is vital that you still know the level of detail required.

- Based on your F1 technical knowledge, you should recognise that we are looking at how to account for brands using IAS 38 Intangible Assets. Given this, there are three key recognition criteria:

  (1) Does the potential intangible asset (here the brand) give rise to future economic benefit?

  (2) Can the cost or fair value of the potential intangible asset be measured reliably?

  (3) Has the potential intangible asset been acquired or is it capable of separation from the business?

- This could form the basis of your plan and, therefore, answer structure.

- Under each criterion you would need to state the rule and then discuss whether or not it has been met and why. It is not enough to say a rule has been met without any explanation or justification.

- Starting with rule 1:

  Technical knowledge – statement of rule

  Does the brand give rise to future economic benefit?

  Application with justification

  "The First Class Bakery brand, especially with its increasing prominence, will give us future economic benefits in terms of revenue and profit. A brand, by definition, engenders customer loyalty and hence continued sales."

  "**Therefore** this criterion would appear to be met.".

- Next, rule 2:

  Technical knowledge – statement of rule

  Can the cost or fair value of the brand be measured reliably?

  Application with justification

  "To place a value on our brand is very subjective. Whilst there are various brand valuation methods and specialist consultants available to undertake such work, such a valuation is unlikely to meet the definition of reliable measurement required by the accounting standard. This is because of the large number of assumptions about the future which would be required."

  "**Therefore** this criterion is not met."

- Then rule 3:

  Technical knowledge – statement of rule

  Has the brand been acquired or is it capable of separation from the business?

  "In order to capitalise the value of a brand, that brand needs to be either acquired from an external source (where there is therefore a reliable measurement base being the consideration paid) or be capable of separation from the rest of the business in the sense that it can be sold."

Application with justification

"In our case, clearly our brand value has been generated through internal means (through the work of our sales team and our marketing efforts) rather than as a result of an acquisition.

In addition, if we were to separate our brand with a view to selling it, we would be left with only the supermarket own label business as we would no longer have the right to use the First Class Bakery name. Indeed, if we sold our name even the own label business could be in jeopardy because our customers are still reliant on the name as a measure of quality."

"Therefore again this criterion is not met."

- Finally, having evaluated each criterion, you will need some form of conclusion:

"Therefore we cannot capitalise the value of our brand in the statement of financial position.

Examiner's comments

The first element of task 3 was generally well answered, which is pleasing giving previous comments about a lack of F1 knowledge.

There were many answers that showed a complete and accurate understanding of IAS 38 as well as an ability to apply the knowledge to the First Class Bakery brand. Indeed, a few answers scored maximum marks, a vast improvement on the performance of candidates on financial reporting sections

5 Final tips

Finally, the examiner has given the following advice for candidates:

- **Application**

  Application to the scenario is key to achieving a good mark.

  Simply reproducing rote-learned answers or pure knowledge of a topic area will score very few, if any, marks.

  Similarly taking a scatter gun approach to an issue and commenting on everything that you know about it from a theoretical point of view will score few marks.

- **Planning**

  When sitting an Operational level case study examination, it is important to take time to plan your answer so that you are able to apply your knowledge to the specifics of the case. I would suggest that for certain tasks you plan your answers in the answer screen itself.

  For example, if you are asked for the potential benefits and problems of outsourcing a particular function, I would suggest that you first note down headings for benefits and problems.

  Then under each heading list your benefits and problems; these will become your sub-headings.

  Then you can write a short paragraph under each sub-heading. This will allow you time to think about all of the points that you want to make and will help to give your answer a clear format.

  Ultimately, it should save you time.

- **The pre-seen material**

  Preparation on the pre-seen material is vital.

  Ensure that you are very familiar with the business, especially the financial information, before the exam as this will help you with applying your knowledge and will save you time.

  Similarly, an awareness of the industry that the business is in will help you to think of the wider issues that might impact on decisions that you could be asked to comment on.

- **Know the whole syllabus**

  The Operational level case study examination covers all of the P1, E1 and F1 syllabi and therefore no topic area is off limits to the examiner.

  Make sure that you do not leave topic areas out of your preparation.

  Given previous comments in this report and other reports, it is evident that F1 knowledge of financial reporting standards is poor. Please pay special attention to this.

- **Technical skills**

  The Operational level case study examination is weighted 64% technical skills.

  It is really important that your technical knowledge is comprehensive so that you can apply it to the scenario you are faced with.

- **Justify your comments**

  Be prepared to give balanced arguments or appraisals.

  Quite often you will be asked whether a tool or technique is appropriate to the business – it is just as likely to be suitable as not suitable.